Sports, Technology, and Madness

A COLLECTION

Connor Groel

CONTENTS

PREFACE

I would like to begin by providing some context and background information for what you are about to read. The following pages contain a collection of pieces I've written and released over the past year. This book comes at an exciting time as I prepare to graduate from the University of Texas at Austin in May. The pieces chosen represent the work I am most proud of and that I feel will remain relevant into the future, even if the event they were written in response to has passed.

In particular, I'm pleased with the diversity of this collection, both in terms of the variety of sports and industry topics discussed, and with the differing styles of the pieces themselves, including theses, speculative fiction, and documentary-style storytelling, along with more traditional editorial and analytical writing. With these pieces, I aim to inform and perhaps challenge you to view elements of sports through a different lens. I truly hope you will enjoy it.

Sports, Technology, and Madness is divided into five sections. The first three consist of what I consider my three major projects of the year, separated by their length and overall scope. The final two sections each consist of a series of individual pieces.

The opening section, entitled *Adapt or Die: Technology is Forever Altering Sports*, is a wide-ranging exploration of the future of the sports industry and how advancements in technology are forcing sports to either adapt to the digital age or risk losing popularity. It marks the culmination of many thematic connected research interests of mine in 2019 and deals with topics such as the mastering of games by artificial intelligence programs, the aesthetic appeal of sports, instant replay, and the sports and games of the future.

Second, *An Overindulgence of Madness* is a fictional piece in the form of an article from the year 2047 published by sportswriter Asher Raines in his column, *Raining Takes*. The article profiles the first annual Summer Madness tournament, a supplementary tournament to March Madness which features 368 teams and takes place entirely within 24 hours. Remember the following: everything that takes place before 2019 is real. Everything afterward is fiction. At least, until it becomes reality...

Last of the major projects is *Out of the Dawg House: The Story of the 2018 Cleveland Browns*, which was originally released in both written form and as an audio documentary for the launch of the *Connor Groel Sports* podcast. The piece details the history of the Cleveland Browns franchise through early successes and modern futility highlighted by a winless season in 2017 and their subsequent attempt at redemption in one of the most eventful and thoroughly unpredictable seasons of all-time.

In the fourth section, *On Rules and Structure,* I tackle questions relating to the rules of sports and the structure of leagues and competitions. Among these topics are the NBA three-point shot, five-set tennis matches, the size of North American sports leagues, the World Chess Championship, and the College Football Playoff.

Finally, the *Best of the Rest* comprises individual pieces unrelated to rules and structure. I discuss why some sports are more popular than others, talk about Andrew Luck's surprise retirement, argue for better treatment of women's sports, calculate the maximum number of home runs a player can hit in a season, explore the greatest ironman streaks in sports history, and more. Pieces in each of the final two sections are organized chronologically.

This collection has been formatted for paperback publication. Minor edits to the content and formatting of pieces have been made. Original versions for all pieces, with sources, graphics, and external links where appropriate can be found at Medium.com/@ConnorGroel. Additionally, feel free to share your comments and interact with me on Twitter @ConnorGroel.

I want to thank everyone who has supported my writing over the years, especially my amazing parents. Publishing a book has long been a dream of mine, and to finally be able to do so is a great feeling. Here's to many more.

I: ADAPT OR DIE: TECHNOLOGY IS FOREVER ALTERING SPORTS

Originally published: December 31, 2019

Introduction

Improvements in technology have been generally celebrated in sports. However, it is time to question the idea that this progress has been for the better. As we enter the 2020s, it is clear that technology presents an existential threat to the modern sports landscape as the root cause of many irreversible changes. Existing sports must adapt to become better suited for this new environment or face the prospect of declining popularity.

To be clear, this is not a theory. These changes are already occurring and have affected nearly every sport and every aspect of sports. What began for me as an exploration of whether advancements in computing and analytics are changing the way sports are played, leading to decreases in overall enjoyment of the industry has extended to other areas. Some of these include the effects of technology on how we consume sports, the integrity of sports, and the types of sports and games we will play and watch in the future.

This is a deep, multifaceted discussion, but every discussion needs a starting point. Let's begin by showing the power of computers and what happens when they become strong enough at a game to beat the best human players - something already seen in mind sports. Many of the current issues in that realm are strongly connected to those in what we would consider traditional sports.

Mind Sports and the Quest to "Solve" Games

When the field of artificial intelligence (AI) became an academic discipline in the 1950s, teaching computers to play games was both an interesting challenge for researchers and a way to measure the progress of these machines. Being perhaps the most famous strategy game of all and one of incredible complexity, chess was naturally of interest.

For decades, computers consistently improved, rising in Elo

rating at a much faster rate than the top human players. The culmination of 40 years of effort came with a pair of six-game matches between Garry Kasparov, the reigning world chess champion, and Deep Blue, a chess-playing computer developed by IBM.

Deep Blue won the first game of their 1996 match, becoming the first computer to defeat a world champion in a classical game under tournament regulations. Kasparov tied the series in game 2 and would take the match 4-2. However, in their rematch the following year, Deep Blue emerged victorious in a decisive sixth game to defeat the world champion 3 ½ - 2 ½.

Immediately following the loss, Kasparov blamed the result on his poor performance rather than the strength of his opponent. Yet, symbolically, the damage was done. The Deep Blue matches garnered significant media attention and were seen as a break-through for artificial intelligence. Some had predicted that computers would never be able to defeat top human players. Deep Blue was a testament to the power of computers. While there was a short period where it was debatable whether man or machine was stronger, by the early 2000s, it became clear that chess computers reigned supreme and were still improving. Humans would never stand a chance again.

That progress is still ongoing as chess engines pass Elo thresh-olds previously thought unachievable. There is still some dis-agreement over whether chess will ever be solved, but as com-puter skill rises, the competition between engines to perfect the game remains healthy.

There may be no more matches between humans and com-puters that are garnering any attention, but in place of that rivalry, chess AI has taken on a new role for humans - that of a training tool.

For the top chess professionals, technology is essential to their study and preparation. Players can review their previous matches with chess engines to determine where they made mistakes and what their best option was on every move. Over time, this helps them develop a better sense of the game. They can also use databases of past matches to study specific opponents and decide which strategies to employ against them in upcoming tournaments. This allows them to train as efficiently as possible.

The increased access to information provided by technology has made today's top human chess players better than ever before. But while this enhanced quality of play is exciting, it has not come without consequences.

During the 2018 World Chess Championship match between reigning titleholder Magnus Carlsen and challenger Fabiano Caruana, all 12 scheduled matches resulted in a draw. This meant the match was forced to go to a set of faster-paced tiebreak games where Carlsen defended his crown.

This high frequency of drawn games was not a one-time occurrence. In Carlsen's previous title defense against Sergey Karjakin, 10 of 12 games were drawn, with the championship again being decided in tiebreakers. Overall, 75% of the games played in the last seven world championship matches have ended in a tie, with a clear trend towards more ties over time.

Beyond just the end results, on a move per move basis, play in these world championship matches has become more precise, with the moves made getting closer to the strongest possible moves. In a similar trend, the differences in quality of play between winning and losing players are closer than ever before, meaning among the world's best, margins are thinner than ever before. This can be attributed to the extreme preparedness of players, who often have a good idea of what type of game will be played before it even begins.

It only makes sense that as the overall skill of players increases, there will be less separating them. With the stakes so high, play becomes more memorized, fewer risks are taken, and more games end as draws. In fact, in 2018, Carlsen, who holds a much larger edge over Caruana in faster games, seemed content to play for draws in the classic games and take the match to tie-breakers.

It's difficult to criticize Carlsen or any other player for acting in ways that give them the best chance at success. That being said, many chess fans criticized the Carlsen-Caruana match as boring, and if decisive results are the mark of exciting play, there is a real reason to be concerned, as we should only expect to see more tight, mostly-drawn games in future iterations of the World Chess Championship.

For me, complaints about the modern state of chess speak to the reason why we play games. The objective of a game is not necessarily to win - often, it's to try to figure out how to win. We create and apply different strategies to test what works and adjust accordingly. The beauty is in the experimentation. At such a high level, much of that experimentation goes away. The closer a game gets to being solved, the less exciting it can be.

Public perception of major chess tournaments is important, as using chess as a main source of income is only viable for a select few professionals. Should the excitement be taken out of the game, companies will be less willing to sponsor individuals and events, interest will wane at the local level, and the support for competitive chess will diminish. With this in mind, it's worth asking whether changes should be made to either the rules of chess or the format of tournaments like the World Chess Championship to prevent draws and increase overall fan appeal.

But chess isn't the only mind sport where technology has made its mark. Artificial intelligence programs have been designed to master many other games, including those of similar or even greater complexity than chess, such as Go. In 2016, AlphaGo, a Go-playing program developed by Google DeepMind, defeated

18-time world champion Lee Sedol four games to one. The following year, a stronger version of AlphaGo defeated current world champion Ke Jie in each of three games, and since, even stronger versions of the program have been developed, with AlphaZero the most recent. This was another huge step for AI, as there are more possible games of Go than atoms in the observable universe. AlphaZero has also shown an ability to beat both top human players and engines in Shogi.

Chess, Go, and Shogi, however, are all games of perfect information, where each player has full knowledge of the game state at any point in time. Poker, on the other hand, is a game of imperfect information, since players are not aware of the cards in their opponents' hands. This has made poker a particularly tricky game for computer programs to play well until recently. (An AI developed by Carnegie Mellon and Facebook AI is currently capable of defeating the top human players, albeit under certain restrictions).

Yet, humans have still made major advancements in strategy, and few sports, if any, have seen such a drastic improvement in quality of play over just the 21st century. Like chess, though, this has come at the viewer's expense.

Many of the boisterous personalities from poker's yesteryear have been replaced with a new-age type of player who plays slower, more methodically, and uses an extensive knowledge of the game's mathematics, rather than playing based on instincts or "feel". They've grown up in an era where online poker, even at the lowest stakes, has become much more difficult, and computer software such as head-up displays (HUDs) allows players to view the tendencies of their opponents and adjust their strictly regimented game plans accordingly.

While not quite as severe as chess, there is once again a lack of experimentation. The game has never been played at such a high level before, but while those familiar with poker can appreciate that complexity, it can simultaneously be easy to watch a silent table of cold, calculating twenty-somethings in hoodies and wonder what happened. While this isn't representative of the entire poker community, it's undeniable that a major shift has taken place.

Measures such as shot clocks and big blind antes have been implemented to improve the pace of play, but more than anything, poker needs interesting personalities to spice up the table. (Having entertaining and recognizable participants is a huge component for the popularity of any sport.) This is much easier with televised cash games, where players are chosen for their personalities and encouraged to put on a show, as opposed to tournaments, which are far more serious in tone.

The stakes have been raised, particularly in the last decade, for tournaments, with the rise of high roller and super high roller tournaments which regularly feature $100,000 buy-ins and have even reached $1 million or more, but at some point, higher stakes won't be enough to garner more watching interest. It's also worth noting that the massive sums of money involved and tighter margins between players could lead to a tense atmosphere and community.

Luckily, poker has several attributes that make it well-positioned for the future. These will be discussed in more detail later, but specifically, the fact that the prize pools are put up by players in the form of buy-ins means poker will stay popular as long as people want to play, and considering how enticing gambling can be, the game is in safe hands.

It's also worth mentioning here that while in chess, there is theoretically always a "best" move to be played, the same cannot be said for poker, due to the imperfect nature of the game and differences in styles between players, which can be affected by many factors even outside of the hand such as the number of players remaining in a tournament and the payout structure.

But for the top players, even if the competitive structure remains, will the motivation be there? This is something I've long wondered about mind sports in particular. We've reached the point where humans will never again beat the top computer programs. Previously, the chess world champion could claim to be exactly that - the best player in the world. That's no longer the case. The same is true for Go and shogi. AI has not surpassed humans in every variant of poker, but that's only because it hasn't been a priority. The fundamentals are in place, and with time and effort, the computer will be king there too.

So, when being the best at a game is impossible, even if you dedicate your entire life to it, will top pros lose interest in competing? Of course, there are other reasons to compete, and some may not be bothered by their inferiority to machines. For a certain type of player, though, it could be very discouraging.

It seems that recently, we have found an example of one such player. Lee Sedol, the Go world champion who lost to AlphaGo back in 2016, retired in November 2019, citing the rise of AI as a primary reason for his decision. "Even if I become number one," he said, "there is an entity that cannot be defeated." As a species, our brains are our greatest asset. Now, humanity's mind sport champions must cope with their permanent inferiority. Anything you can do, AI can do better.

Opportunities for AI in Traditional Sports

Artificial intelligence has already made its mark on mind sports, but there may be opportunities for AI to break into traditional sports as well. To illustrate this, I'd like to start by briefly touching on esports.

As mind sports have been solved, and a similar trend has occurred in esports. Notably, OpenAI's team of five neural networks appropriately named "OpenAI Five" was able to beat OG, the greatest Dota 2 team in the world, and Google DeepMind's

AlphaStar program has recently reached the grandmaster level in the real-time strategy game StarCraft II and is capable of beating 99.8% of human players. AIs have shown themselves to be elite in many other games as well.

These video games feature nonstop, simultaneous action by competing parties. They can contain many playable characters, each with a unique skill set, and require the development of strategies to achieve short and long-term goals. This requires both the skill and understanding to complete several different actions per second and the ability to adapt to a constantly changing game state. Games involving multiple players on a team additionally force players to cooperate to coordinate actions.

There is effectively an infinite amount of ways a match can play out. This range of possible outcomes and overall complexity is comparable to traditional sports. There might not be perfect solutions to every situation, as these are imperfect games, but if computers can strategize better than humans in an esports environment, who's to say the same thing won't happen in traditional sports?

Esports startup Gosu.ai is an AI video game coach which currently is available to help gamers at League of Legends, Dota 2, and PlayerUnknown's Battlegrounds (PUBG). It works by watching a user's matches and then sending them post-match analytics and analysis which allows them to improve their game. Recently, the company has announced a voice assistant for League of Legends which will provide in-game advice as well.

This particular AI is likely years away from being used in a professional capacity, but using artificial intelligence in coaching seems like an inevitability, both in and outside of esports. It would be more difficult to implement in games with constant action, but in sports like baseball or football, which are comprised of individual pitches or plays, AI could be used as a play-caller.

In baseball, this means learning from the tendencies of opposing players to tell pitchers what pitches to throw, fielders where to position themselves, and batters what they are likely to face. Based on personnel and game state, football plays could be called to maximize a team's chances of winning.

In the Madden video game series, players are offered suggestions on what plays to run based off of this same information. Factor in an understanding of the opposition's tendencies, and I don't think it's a stretch to suggest that AI could call plays better than NFL head coaches and coordinators in the near future, if not immediately.

All sports should be working on developing AI for similar purposes. This wouldn't necessarily put coaches out of work - they'd still get the final say on decision-making and would be necessary for leadership, emotional support, and help with the mental game, not to mention practice and training, among a host of other things. It would, however, maximize a team's chances on the field, which, of course, is the bottom line in the sports industry.

Let's look beyond coaching - could AI be the athletes of the future? In the future, will we watch robots play sports?

One could argue that we already do. Both the Top Chess Engine Competition (TCEC) and Chess.com's Computer Chess Championship (CCC) are competitions between the best chess engines in the world that are streamed live online. The Computer Olympiad similarly pits computer programs against each other in a variety of games.

However, these events are incredibly niche. We're still a far cry from a mainstream sporting experience where people tune into watch their favorite algorithms duke it out. Down the line, this remains a possibility, but the sport in question would have to feature gameplay more easily understandable than something like chess.

For example, the average person would be unable to understand a chess match between the Stockfish and Komodo engines. Even for those familiar with chess, the engines perform at such a high level that it is impossible to fully understand their strategies.

While only a select few people are capable of grasping the full capabilities of computers, human greatness is far more evident. In a game of basketball, even if a viewer cannot perform the actions they are watching, it is not difficult to comprehend what is occurring. Any robot vs. robot competition would require this element of intelligibility.

Naturally, this leads to the idea of robots playing these sports which already have large fan bases. As a whole, a sport like basketball would be one of the hardest for robots to master, specifically in terms of the motion involved. They are, however, capable of shooting the ball incredibly effectively from a set position. Robots are skilled at these precise movements, and their ability to remain steady has made them valuable in the manufacturing and medical industries, among others. This means that there are some sports such as archery and darts where robots are already capable of surpassing humans.

So why don't we watch robot archery? Outside of the regulations preventing robots from participating in competitions such as the Olympics, one reason is that we don't want to see perfection. It's boring.

Humans may strive for perfection, but that's only because it is unattainable. There will always be ways for us to get better. The human idea of perfection is really about continual improvement. On the other hand, robots can be programmed to never miss. For watching someone (or something) succeed to be interesting, the possibility of failure must exist.

In many individual pursuits, failure can be just about eliminated in robots. This is what makes the concept of head-to-head competition so exciting, as not every participant can win. I would expect to see effort made over the coming decades to create robots capable of playing these types of sports. Still, I'm unsure of how appealing watching these competitions would be.

All competition between robots is missing the emotional element. As humans, we want to know our athletes' backgrounds - their journey to reach the present moment. That contains the successes along with the struggles and sacrifices. We want to see their emotions and learn about their personalities.

We want to see the pinnacle of human achievement. For us, there is a difference between having the right skills and strategy and being able to execute. Even if robots are better overall, being able to perform and to be the best on any given day will always be interesting.

Perhaps we will see an increase in competitions that blend elements of traditional sports with technology, such as in combat robotics and drone racing. This could even lead to humans controlling robots in sports like basketball or soccer as if they were real-life video games. At least in these scenarios, the humans behind the machines are more prominent and actually involved in the game. This visibility allows for more opportunities to create stories. For now, though, more opportunities seem to exist behind the scenes rather than on the field.

Aesthetics, Pace of Play, and the Viewing Experience

Even if robots aren't taking over the roles of athletes, technology is still having a huge impact on the viewing experience of sports. The analytics movement has led to major shifts in the way sports are played which have made games slower-paced and less aesthetically pleasing, while the development of new entertainment options over time has created barriers to live sports and more appealing alternatives to them.

The rise of advanced statistics in sports begins with baseball. Bill James got the ball rolling with his annual *Baseball Abstract*, and the idea of maximizing efficiency hit the mainstream with Billy Beane and the *Moneyball* A's. No major sport, though, has been as affected by the rise of analytics than basketball, and it all has to do with the three-point shot.

During the 1979-80 NBA season, the first year with a three-point line, teams attempted an average of just 2.8 threes per game. It would take another eight seasons before that number reached even five per game. In the early days of the three, the shot was mainly reserved for late-game situations and desperate, end of shot clock heaves.

Over time, players who grew up in the three-point era entered the league and shot from long-distance from a higher rate. Still, the shot was highly underutilized when compared to its potential effectiveness. The NBA managed to entice more threes by moving the line in for a few years in the mid-90s, but when the line returned to its original place, attempts from behind the line dipped, and wouldn't return to the same level for another decade.

It wasn't until the 2010s that the NBA uncovered the true value of the three. NBA shot tracking data and visualization from Kirk Goldsberry showed that by far, the most efficient places to shoot the ball are from under the basket and behind the three-point line.

Surprisingly, once you get beyond about five feet from the basket, shooting percentages from each distance are highly consistent out to about 25 feet, all between about 35 and 40%. The only difference between them is that some of the shots are worth an entire extra point. By minimizing shots taken in the mid-range and focusing on more threes to go along with layups and free throws, the most valuable shot of all, teams could increase their offensive efficiency.

The NBA took note, and as if a switch was flipped, three-point attempts ballooned in the 2010s from 18.0 by each team per game in 2010-11 to 32.0 (36.9% of all shot attempts) in the 2018-19 season. We now see a three-pointer every 45 seconds during a game, with the long-range explosion showing no signs of slowing down.

Modern basketball is as mathematically optimal as ever. Yet, there is a growing number of people displeased with the NBA's on-court product. At times, the game feels like a glorified three-point shootout with little actual skill as players chuck the deep ball back and forth while simultaneously attempting to draw fouls by any means necessary.

It's easy to characterize the changes in basketball this decade by what we've gained in terms of increases in three-point shot attempts, but it may be more telling to examine the situation in terms of what we've lost. With the rise in threes, there has been a drastic decline in the mid-range game and the post game.

These shifts have disproportionately affected the power forward and center positions. Traditionally used to playing in and around the paint, these positions are now being asked to develop an outside shot and forced to defend on the perimeter. Big men now have to be more capable ball handlers, and their rebounding edge has taken a hit from the longer rebounds that come from three-point attempts.

In this NBA, the ability to shoot from three and handle like a guard are practically prerequisites for every position. As a result, the traditional big man has become a dying breed, in favor of positionless basketball and small ball. The NBA is trending towards a game where every player looks and plays similar to each other. Math has dictated that there are right and wrong ways to play basketball, and diversity will be sacrificed for efficiency.

If the rise of analytics is destroying old ways of playing basketball, the Houston Rockets are the Grim Reaper. Under general manager Daryl Morey, the Rockets have embraced analytics more so than any other franchise with an approach to the game dubbed "Moreyball".

From the philosophy of head coach Mike D'Antoni to the playing style of superstar James Harden and construction of the entire roster, Houston has borderline religiously sought out maximizing offensive efficiency. During the 2017-18 season, the Rockets became the first team in the history of the NBA to shoot more threes than twos, something they repeated in 2019 by averaging 45.4 three-point attempts per game. Harden took more than 13 of those himself and has also averaged double-digit free throw attempts in six of his first seven seasons with the team.

Granted, some people enjoy the analytical masterclass of Rockets basketball, but as time goes on, more and more fans see them as boring or frustrating to watch. When the team, and Harden, in particular, is hot, it can be exciting. But when they go cold, things get ugly quickly. Considering that it seems inevitable that every team will soon look like the Rockets, this doesn't spell good things for the NBA.

This situation is interesting because until very recently, the three-pointer was seen as one of the most thrilling things in sports. Stephen Curry transformed the game with his shooting ability and remains incredibly popular despite his game being mimicked throughout the league.

The difference is that with Curry, not only was he the first person to really weaponize the three-point shot, he also happens to be the greatest shooter in the history of the league. In his record-shattering 2015-16 season where he made 402 threes, Curry shot better from behind the arc (45.4%) than the NBA as a whole on all shots (45.2%). It was Curry's transformative shooting ability that led to his popularity, not simply the fact that he shot tons of threes.

There is nothing transformative about the Rockets taking loads of three-pointers. Instead of shooting so well one can't take their eyes off them, the Rockets simply take a ton of threes and convert at a rate just good enough to make it better than any other strategy. NBA teams have realized that when everyone knows how valuable the three is, it's practically impossible to win playing certain other styles of basketball.

This is what fans don't like. To briefly return to chess, play at the highest level has become boring because there is less experimentation and differences between players. The NBA is experiencing a similar issue. Fans want there to be potential for players and teams of different skill sets to succeed. The players who in previous eras would be the most dominant inside players are now spotting up from 25 feet away from the basket.

Shooting a high-volume of three-pointers might lead to the most efficient offense in the modern NBA, but what is mathematically optimal is not necessarily the most aesthetically pleasing.

There is beauty in the suboptimal. So many of our most memorable moments in sports come from ill-advised decisions, unique occurrences, and high degree of difficulty successes. We love spontaneity, randomness, and the things you can't draw up in a playbook. In chasing the optimal, we lose these things.

Just as with basketball, baseball has experienced a decline in diversity in favor of the analytically superior. Recent years have seen surges in what are known as the three true outcomes - home runs, walks, and strikeouts. The most efficient offenses specialize in the former two, while the latter comes as a consequence of trying to achieve them. Players are more reluctant to swing their bat in hopes of earning a base on balls, but when they do swing, it's for the fences.

The three true outcomes got their name because they don't require action from any of the defenders outside of the pitcher and catcher. A rise in these outcomes means fewer balls in play and less overall action.

Along with drops in action, analytics have led to longer game times and slower pace of play. Added patience from batters means that the average plate appearance features more pitches. Additionally, an increase in pitching changes over time to both manage pitcher health and create more favorable matchups against batters has extended the length of games.

Pace of play has been a major talking point in not only baseball but also a number of other sports. The shot clock, an idea which started in basketball to manage pace of play, has already been adapted in sports such as football (called the play clock), certain poker tournaments, and minor league baseball in the form of a pitch clock. The MLB is likely to add a pitch clock in the near future, and even golf is starting to toy with the idea of a shot clock.

Working to reduce average game lengths in sports is a good idea, but I wonder how much of the problem is less a result of the games themselves and more a consequence of technological influences outside of them.

In 2019, the average MLB regular season game was three hours and 10 minutes long. 100 years ago, that number would be under two hours. In fact, six out of eight games in the 1919 World Series lasted one hour and 47 minutes or shorter. Yes, that was at the end of the Dead Ball Era, and there have since been rule changes to increase offense and the adoption of strategies that have made games longer. Still, this only accounts for a portion of the difference.

Those games were played before the television, and thus featured very few stoppages in play. In contrast, the average MLB broadcast today features at least 45 minutes of commercials.

Even when games were televised, though, baseball was the most popular sport in the U.S. for a long time. The biggest difference between then and now is competition. Back in, say, the 1960s or 70s, people were more willing to sit down and watch an entire baseball game because fewer things were competing for their attention. There were once only three or four TV channels. Now, there are hundreds.

In the 21st century, computers, smartphones, and other devices provide almost unlimited entertainment options. The world is more connected and fast-paced than ever, and we're doing other things than watching sports. Even when we decide to tune in, we're doing so in different ways.

How Are We Watching?

When was the last time a sports event had your full, undivided attention? I don't mean that you watched part of a game or even an entire game. When was the last time you watched a game start to finish without checking your phone, going on the internet, or doing another task?

I'd guess that it's been a while. In 2019, live sports are never the only thing going on. But then again, neither is anything else. There is always something else to be watching, playing, doing, and rarely can any singular stimulus captivate someone for an extended period of time.

Often, sports are reduced to background noise. If the bases are loaded, or if a football team is in the red zone, we'll check out what's happening. Otherwise, the game will be on just to have something on. Sports are different than most other types of programming in that you don't need to be actively watching - with just a glance, it's possible to understand the situation.

The ability to have a second device handy while watching sports has changed the experience tremendously, even if just allowing someone to follow the game on social media or look up stats. But now, with the rise of streaming games (both legally and illegally), those devices are far more than just supplements. They're becoming the experience themselves, which threatens the stability of the television industry and will have a major impact on the business of sports.

As more and more people have cut the cord in recent years and episodic series have lost favor to on-demand platforms like Netflix, live sports have kept the television industry afloat as the last major source of appointment TV. However, as the cord-cutting trend continues, particularly with the younger generations, it will be increasingly difficult for television networks to generate viewers, even with the sports programs traditionally seen as guaranteed moneymakers.

To be clear, sports will not move away from TV any time soon, and I still personally believe that rumors of the death of cable are somewhat exaggerated. However, this could lead to some very interesting developments in the next round of media rights deals.

The current television contracts for most major sports expire in the early 2020s, which means that the next few years of negotiations will set the stage for the future of sports broadcasting. Since games started being televised, TV rights deals have only increased in value. However, it's very much up in the air if that will continue. Will decreasing ratings mean shorter and less valuable contracts, or will sports' arguably stronger position against other types of programming which have been more affected by cord-cutting mean sports are actually more valuable?

For the first time in history, media revenue now represents the largest share of total revenue in sports, surpassing ticket sales. This makes these media rights deals incredibly important for leagues. Luckily, there is no shortage of companies looking to get involved.

Over the last few years, companies such as Amazon, Facebook, and Twitter, along with over-the-top (OTT) services like YouTube TV, Hulu, and ESPN+, have experimented with streaming live sports. It seems likely that the next round of media rights deals will include both television and streaming contracts for all the major packages to maximize revenue for the leagues and keep as many players as possible interested in moving forward. In addition, leagues will continue trying to tap into international markets to expand their reach and potential audience.

At some point, someone like Amazon might look to make a bid for exclusive rights to something like Thursday Night Football, but in the present, TV remains a far more accessible option, especially for older viewers who make up a large percentage of the NFL's audience and may not want or be able to watch the game on another platform. We're still probably a minimum of a few decades away from a total pivot to streaming.

But even with more ways to watch games than ever before, some sports are struggling to get people to care. The greatest thing the NFL has going for it is its ability to dominate an entire day of the week. With just 16 regular season games, every game truly matters, so fans are eager to tune into their favorite team and any other big matchups. The NBA and NHL, with 82-game schedules, and the MLB, with 162 games, are unable to generate as much hype for each game.

In our busy lives, chances are that we won't choose to watch a game if doing so doesn't feel essential. The NBA is in a particularly interesting situation, where a high percentage of people who consider themselves fans of the league don't watch many games, particularly in the regular season. They'll follow the major storylines and view highlights but be much more of a passive fan until playoff time.

The NBA has done so well at creating storylines around things like social media beef and offseason speculation that what's happening off the court is often more interesting than what's happening on it. Other leagues can learn a lot from the NBA's marketing efforts. Meanwhile, the NBA is working on maximizing entertainment throughout the season, which has led to ideas such as the midseason tournament.

There's Nothing "Instant" About Replay

In such a crowded media environment, all leagues should be focused on making their product as strong as possible. One area which receives constant criticism as a result of the evolution of technology is that of officiating and replay review.

What began in the 1960s as a way to fill time in between football snaps and show action which had previously taken place away from the ball has since been incorporated in all major sports as a way to ensure officials get the important calls right.

Over time, the use of replay has expanded in both overall scope (the types of plays that can be reviewed) and frequency. New technologies are being developed to provide more accurate camera angles and we've seen the addition of extra officials and off-site replay centers to aid in review and TV rules analysts to provide explanations to the viewing audience.

Despite all of these precautions, the officiating process has never been more scrutinized than today. Partially, this is because the process is still far too inefficient, causing long stoppages in play. This can halt a team's momentum and kill the mood in big situations. Instead of celebrating after a game-winning touchdown, teams now often have to wait a few minutes to learn if the play will stand.

The other major problem comes in the form of expectations. Previously, we were forced to acknowledge that without review, some officiating mistakes would be made, as no one is perfect. However, with the emphasis that has been placed on review, both players and fans now expect perfection and feel cheated when a missed call goes against them, leading to conspiracies about outcomes being rigged.

Modern TV broadcasts allow us to see high-quality, slow-motion replays from multiple angles. This turns everyone into an expert liable to outraged at any perceived errors. And with the oftentimes ambiguous standards needed to reverse a call upon further review, situations frequently arise where fans of both teams feel confident that the call should favor them.

NBA commissioner Adam Silver believes that with the emergence of new technology, the league cannot turn the clock back on transparency. This has led them to prioritize doing everything in their power to improve officiating and publish mistakes made late in games. But at some point, it becomes a lot of work for negligible gains that seem to actually hurt the viewing experience.

Even if officiating is better than ever before, humans will always make mistakes. TV forces us to see those mistakes, and as overall accuracy improves, we get angrier and more suspicious of the errors that do occur. This leads to the expansion of review that harms pace of play without fully solving the problem. It's an unbreakable cycle. The league can't win.

As controversial an opinion as this may be, I believe replay review should be eliminated from sports. In its current form, not every call is allowed to be reviewed (baseball umpires are surprisingly poor at calling balls and strikes, although these decisions are unreviewable), and some sports feature limits on how many calls can be challenged or limit reviews to certain points in the game.

This system treats some calls as more important than others, a necessary evil as it's not feasible to review every single call made in a game. But if you can't review everything, should review really exist at all?

In theory, missed calls should go against both sides and balance out over the course of a game, much less a season. Replay review might make officiating in sports more accurate, but it doesn't make it fairer. Eliminating it entirely would serve to restore the social contract between players and referees, who were added to be impartial adjudicators of the rules. At one time, the referee had full authority. Replay has taken that away, leading to the disparagement of game officials.

At a point in time where replay is constantly expanding, I think it should be stripped back, perhaps with the exception of tennis, where the Hawkeye system achieves near-perfection in just seconds while blending naturally into the broadcast.

We will reach a point, however, where robots can perform the job of an official better than humans without added delay. At that point, and only at that point, a sport should make the switch to robots. The Atlantic League tested having a robot umpire call balls and strikes this past season, and I would like to see Major League Baseball work to improve that technology and implement it in the coming years.

Umpires and officials in all sports will still be needed as backup as well as to help manage the game and make certain calls robots are not capable of, but certain aspects of the job could certainly be optimized. We would have to be careful, though, with how much control we give. In the NFL, for instance, there is holding on virtually every play, but we can't penalize each one. Situations like this may also work better using human discretion.

The only reason why leagues may be hesitant to embrace automated officiating, should it be quick and more accurate than humans would be the potential backlash by fans over the potential of these robots being rigged or somehow able to hack. Even if these concerns are unfounded, the perception could be deadly.

Ethics and Cheating

Any possible way to cheat or rig a sports event marks a threat to the entire industry. Competitive integrity is taken so seriously because the core of sports lies in the idea of an uncertain outcome. Everyone plays by the same rules on an equal playing field, and the best player or team wins. Unlike other scripted forms of entertainment, anything can happen.

However, new technologies make it easier for people to gain an unfair advantage, which is perhaps the single scariest aspect of the rise of technology in sports. This was most visible in one of the biggest sports stories of 2019, the Houston Astros sign-stealing scandal.

This past November, Ken Rosenthal and Evan Drellich of The Athletic broke the story that the Astros illegally stole signs during the 2017 season. According to the report, which was supported by several people who were then employed by the Astros, including pitcher Mike Fiers, the team used a camera in the outfield focused on the opposing catcher to send a live video feed to a monitor positioned in a hallway between the Astros' dugout and clubhouse. Team employees and players would then watch the feed, attempting to decipher the catcher's signs. Once they had done so, they would relay that information to Astros batters by banging on a trash can next to the monitor to indicate off-speed pitches. The process was nearly instantaneous, allowing batters to receive the information before the pitch was thrown.

The story blew up because the Astros won the World Series in 2017. This would mean that they cheated on the way to winning a championship. Over the following days, evidence started to pile up against the team, including a leaked email from a team executive asking scouts for help stealing signs which mentioned the potential use of a camera. On the internet, baseball fans such as Jomboy went back through recordings of Astros home games to find clearly audible banging which perfectly aligned with off-speed pitches. Rob Arthur even managed to analyze game audio to pinpoint the time the banging started (May 19th) and prove that from that point on, the Astros' offense improved.

While it hasn't been proven that the Astros cheating during the 2017 playoffs, it seems likely that if the strategy was effective, they wouldn't have stopped using it altogether, but rather found a better way to decode it. To this point, there have been rumors of the Astros using varied whistles or even having players wear electronic buzzers that look like bandages to convey pitch information.

The entire scandal is insane and appears to have been known about in every level of the organization. Major League Baseball is currently conducting a wide-reaching investigation of the matter and depending on the findings and whether it extended into the 2018 and 2019 seasons, I would expect huge penalties for the team, including fines, a loss of draft picks, suspension and possible bans for coaches and front office members, and potentially even suspensions for players.

However, reports from around the league suggest that while the Astros may have pioneered the video camera technique, illegal sign-stealing is a common practice in several other MLB organizations. Notably, the Boston Red Sox were caught and fined for using an Apple Watch to steal signs during a 2017 series against the New York Yankees. The act of trying to decipher catcher signs is not new, nor is it against the rules. However, doing so through the use of technology makes it illegal, and it has become clear that there are more creative ways to do this than ever before.

The entire situation with sign-stealing around the league is highly troubling. It's also heavily reminiscent of another huge scandal that came to light earlier in the fall when the poker world was rocked by the allegations against Mike Postle.

Postle was a regular player in the cash games broadcast live on Twitch from the Stones Gambling Hall in California. On the stream, he had earned the reputation of having godlike skills by routinely making incredible decisions that seem unfathomable to anyone with an understanding of the game on the way to winning an estimated $250,000.

Stones employee and stream commentator Veronica Brill privately voiced concerns about Postle's play to Stones management before finally going public with the story, releasing a highlight tape of some of Postle's most superhuman plays and contacting popular poker player and content creator Joe Ingram.

Ingram began to watch the footage and was instantly shocked by what seemed to be the greatest player he'd ever seen. But suspicions quickly mounted as Postle never made a major error while always sitting in the same seat and looking down at his phone positioned in between his legs during significant pots.

Immediately, Ingram began hosting daily livestreams where he would watch and discuss Postle's hands while encouraging discussion on the potential cheating methods used. In a very similar way to how the internet investigated the Astros, people became hooked to the story and turned into amateur sleuths. They figured out when he started cheating and began to piece together how it was done, including how Postle used bone conduction technology in a hat to adjust to a rule preventing phone use at the table, along the way determining that someone on the stream's production team must have been aiding him. Currently, there is a lawsuit against Postle featuring many of his opponents as the plaintiff.

Cheating in sports is nothing new. Notable examples include game rigging in the 1919 World Series and in the NBA with referee Tim Donaghy, the steroid era in baseball, and Lance Armstrong's doping scandal. However, technology allows for more clever ways to get away with it.

Unfortunately, the incentive to cheat will always be there. The stakes are simply too high and have only increased as sports have become more lucrative. If people can cheat, they will. Technology provides the "can", and because of that, we must always be on the lookout.

Author's Note: As I perform the last round of edits, Major League Baseball is in a frenzied state. The Astros were fined $5 million and docked top draft picks for the sign-stealing scandal, while manager A.J. Hinch and general manager Jeff Luhnow were suspended from baseball for one year and subsequently fired by the team. Two additional managers (the Red Sox' Alex Cora and the Mets' Carlos Beltrán, who were with the Astros in 2017, have also been fired.) I happen to be of the opinion that the Astros' punishment was on the lighter side, although there are many on both sides of that argument. Particularly troubling to me is the fact that the ruling does nothing to disincentivize the players themselves from cheating.

MLB still has an ongoing investigation into the Red Sox, and at least seven or eight additional teams were mentioned during the Astros investigation for illegal sign-stealing. Questions also remain surrounding the wearable buzzers.

There is still much more to be settled, but the takeaway here is how easy and effective cheating has become with the use of technology. It goes beyond the Astros and beyond baseball as a whole, threatening the integrity of sports.

What Are the Sports and Games of the Future?

So far, we've discussed a variety of ways technology has already impacted and will continue to impact sports. Now, it's time to zoom out and look at the big picture. The world is changing rapidly, and some sports are better positioned than others to adapt and succeed moving forward. Which sports will grow in popularity? Which will fall? What sports and games will we play in the future?

Before we begin, it's worth mentioning that the sports of the future may not even exist yet. A category like esports, which has exploded in popularity so far in the 21st century and seems poised to continue to grow and break into the mainstream, is only possible because of the technology used to create the games. Who knows what will be possible in the future? Could sports utilizing virtual reality be the next big thing? Only time will tell.

As for the sports which are currently popular, though, soccer seems the safest bet to continue to be played and watched for the foreseeable future. Soccer has true global popularity that is unmatched by any other sport. For this reason, it is sometimes referred to as "the world's game". It is incredibly simple and accessible, requiring just a ball, yet requires such complex, precise movements, and team coordination that it seems in no danger of being taken over by robots.

The RoboCup, an annual autonomous robot soccer competition, has the stated goal of producing a team of humanoid robots that can beat the World Cup champion team by 2050, but I'm skeptical of that goal being achieved. Even if that were to occur, soccer has such a deeply rooted history and widespread appeal that I don't think there would be much of an effect on the game.

Basketball also seems to have a strong future led by the growing global nature of the game. In terms of widespread popularity, basketball is arguably the second-most popular sport in the world. Similar to soccer, it benefits from requiring no special equipment outside of a ball and a hoop and features fast-moving action without being a full-contact sport. There is significant potential for growth of the women's game, and the upcoming Basketball Africa League organized by the NBA and FIBA will help the sport reach a massive, relatively untapped market.

When considering the sports likely to decline in popularity down the road, the obvious starting point is football. It may be the most-watched sport in the United States today but make no mistake - football has passed its peak. The CTE findings are incredibly scary, and in an effort to survive, football will have to continue making changes to the rules to make the game safer. Some would argue that alone is tantamount to killing the game, but don't be surprised if a professional flag football league gains support at some point.

Youth participation is declining, which may harm the overall talent pool, and younger generations increasingly seem to favor other sports. Moreover, football does not have the global reach of many other sports despite there being more international fans that one might expect. Even with the compounding threats facing football, there likely won't be any major changes in the next 20 or 30 years due to a highly loyal existing fanbase. After that, however, it's all up in the air.

Baseball will have to deal with its pace of play concerns, but I expect the sport to hold relatively steady moving forward. People have warned of the death of baseball for over a century, yet it's still around, and actually had record revenues in 2019.

Generally, I also think Olympic sports, including track & field, swimming, and gymnastics will remain similar in popularity to their current state. Since the whole concept of the Olympics revolves around finding the best athletes in the world, these sports should be relatively unaffected by technology and artificial intelligence. The main concern here is steroid use.

Despite a generally strong televised product, ice hockey is positioned poorly due to heavy barriers to entry. Most people don't grow up with the sport, and thus are unlikely to become fans later in life. From a playing perspective, it's an expensive sport to get into, and in a world facing a climate change crisis, having a playing surface made of ice isn't particularly ideal. Similar sports like field hockey and lacrosse could rise in popularity from being both safer and played on grass.

Combat sports like boxing and mixed martial arts are tricky. In continuing the theme, these sports have both global reach and accessibility. They also have the advantage of featuring varied strategies based on the background of each competitor. Everyone has different strengths, and since fights feature constant motion, it is impossible to be prepared for everything.

In a world so sanitized and far removed from our evolutionary past, there is something primitive and instinctual that these sports appeal to. Very few things can draw as much interest as a highly anticipated title fight, and Floyd Mayweather was the highest-paid athlete of this decade.

However, there are certainly some major safety concerns. An average of 13 boxers die in the ring each year, and we are beginning to understand the long-term effects of head injuries. Similar to the NFL, these sports could see declines in participation due to this. Additionally, cultural changes in the 21st century might make the idea of contact sports less attractive. Perhaps at no point in human history have aggression and physical domination been less valued in society than in the present. If anything, the designers of combat robots might be more appreciated, leading to a future of fighting shaped by machines in the ring.

Finally, let's return to gambling and esports. I believe that poker and other forms of gambling including sports betting and daily fantasy sports are safer bets to succeed in the future than any individual esport. As I mentioned when discussing poker, the fact that the prize pools are generated by the players in these activities means they have more stability than many esports competitions that rely on sponsor or fan-generated prize pools. Additionally, the fact that gambling activities are open to anyone (assuming it is legal in the area and the person meets the age requirement), likely to become legalized in many states in the near future, and involve elements of luck all work in their favor.

Esports are interesting because while on an industry level the support clearly exists, technology over time has generally made the most popular games outdated within years. No esport has shown an ability to remain professionally relevant for multiple decades, and while that is partially due to the young age of the industry, the coming years will be instrumental in determining both the lifespan of a game and arguably more interesting, the maximum lifespan of a professional esports athlete, since reaction time and technical skill begin declining at a young age.

As certain sports fall and increased access to technology and resources grow the potential audience for sport in general, some sports will rise to fill the void. They may already exist, or they might be created in the future. Either way, what attributes are most important for these sports to have?

Topping the list for me is accessibility. People have to be able to play the sport. Even some of the most popular competitive video games, including League of Legends, Dota 2, and Fortnite are free to play, earning revenue through sponsorships and in-game purchases. Beyond that, people also have to be able to watch the sport. Television deals are important, but in the future and particularly for emerging sports, having free stream options may be even more important. I love how Riot Games has assumed total control of the production of most League of Legends broadcasts and streams live on popular platforms like Twitch and YouTube.

After that, having a fast-paced and aesthetically pleasing product suited for a digital world full of competing content is greatly important. The most underrated skill of all might be storytelling. There need to be stakes - we have to feel something while we're watching. Rivalries are a great way to do this, and if you can get fans to care about teams, those rivalries can become permanent, lasting beyond individual players. At the end of the day, sports are entertainment. Those that can craft the best stories will rise to the top.

The "Unsolvable" Game

Whether it be in chess, poker, basketball, or baseball, a clear trend has emerged in the 21st century. The solving of games and subsequent implementation of analytically superior strategies has led to less interesting gameplay, particularly from the viewer's perspective. When optimal play becomes the goal, there is less room for experimentation. This stifles diversity and creativity, leaving games dull and predictable.

However, the players should not be blamed for this turn of events. They simply act in ways that give them the best chance of winning. Changing the rules to encourage suboptimal behavior is both illogical and contrived. The problem lies within the games themselves, whose complexity is no longer sufficient when pitted against modern computers.

As long as there is a correct way to play a game, this issue will eventually occur. Instead of fighting a losing battle, what would happen if we could create a game that has no optimal strategy? I propose a new type of competition, the true sport of the future: the unsolvable game.

For the unsolvable game to even exist, it has to involve something that cannot be optimized by computers. That is the social element and the unpredictability of human behavior. Unsolvable games are social games that require logical and strategic thinking, but also the ability to communicate effectively with other people. To make bonds and garner trust. To lie and persuade. These are things that robots can't do. Unsolvable games require their players to use the skills that make us human.

There are two main keys to unsolvable games that set them apart. First, there are external forces that prevent a player from ever having complete control of the game. In chess, if a player makes the optimal move in every situation, they are guaranteed at least a draw. Due to a combination of luck and the decisions of other players, this is not true of unsolvable games. There is no way to guarantee victory.

Second, unsolvable games lack a single dominant strategy that can be used regardless of the actions taken by opponents. While it lacks the complexity to be played seriously, rock-paper-scissors is an unsolvable game. No matter which option a player chooses to throw, there is always a counter. In these games, it is impossible to defend against every potential opposing strategy. Even if someone managed to perfect every facet of the game, that very fact would be to their disadvantage.

The best example we currently have of the unsolvable game is the reality television series "Survivor". In the show, groups of between 16-20 people are stranded on an island and divided up into tribes. They must work together to build a shelter and get along with each other while regularly competing in challenges against the other tribe(s). Losing tribes are sent to tribal council where they must vote to eliminate one of their members from the game. In the middle of the game, the tribes are merged, and it becomes every man for themselves.

Let's view the game through the lens of our two keys. First, there is no such thing as control in Survivor. Players are reliant on their tribemates for success in challenges, and at tribal council, everyone gets a vote. Unannounced tribe swaps can instantly change the dynamics of the game, and advantages such as immunity idols and vote steals add more hidden variables primed to shake things up. Even if one player managed to win every challenge for an entire season, the real beauty of Survivor comes in the final twist. When only two or three players remain in the game, they must face a jury of their voted-out peers who decide the winner.

Additionally, Survivor has no dominant strategy. The larger game of Survivor can be condensed into three major parts: the physical game, the mental game, and the social game. Players can be voted out for being too skilled or poor at any of them. You can be perceived as a threat for being too strong or seen as a liability to your tribe for being weak in challenges. Sometimes people are seen as too likable; other times, being an annoyance or an outcast is enough to get voted out. Smart and manipulative people are incredibly dangerous, but if you don't form strong alliances or pick the right allies, your days might be numbered.

Every person playing the game is trying to do whatever it takes to get them closer to the end. There are countless different ways to play, but in most cases, it's important not to be seen as too great of a threat. It's difficult because you want to play as strong a game as possible, but that strength has to go under the radar. And, of course, you never know what other people are thinking.

Unfortunately, only a small group of people will ever get the opportunity to play Survivor. We need to find more accessible games that feature similar elements, and I think we already have with the rise of social deduction or hidden role games.

These games, which are typically played as board or card games, feature players competing either individually or on teams working to achieve competing goals. The trick is that not everyone knows what team everyone is on, or in some cases what cards or abilities they possess. Over the duration of the game, players must achieve their goals while also deducing everyone's true identity or attempting to trick their opponents.

I believe the opportunity exists in the future for these types of social games to continue rising in popularity, perhaps even to the level of sport. One possible hiccup, however, could come from the nature of variance. With any game that features a certain level of luck and unpredictability, it is impossible for the most skilled player to win every time. Determining a champion requires an extended sample size, and even then, the relative strengths of participants may be difficult to determine. This might detract from viewer appeal. Do social deduction games have too much variance to be spectator sports?

Chess is a game purely of skill. Matches between two players may have varying results, but that comes down to who played better. I see Scrabble as a good parallel to chess in the sense that they are both mind sports with competitive circuits and highly skilled top players. The major difference between them is that Scrabble includes an element of luck with the drawing of tiles. One player could draw tiles with higher scoring potential, and neither player knows what tiles the other has. This means that even the best players routinely lose matches, although it typically evens out throughout an entire tournament.

Social deduction games are like Scrabble, except arguably more entertaining. They also completely eliminate the potential for a draw. The success of these games as sports largely depends on finding a balanced game with a strong concept and the right level of variance and then being able to construct the right narratives around it with entertaining players. Once again, sports and games are for entertainment. If we can satisfy that need by constructing games that have unlimited playability due to their unsolvable nature, we could usher in a new wave of entertainment.

Choice: The Greatest Threat to Sports

Throughout this piece, we've examined sports in the context of how they have been changed by technology and how they will continue to adapt to a new age. This entire argument makes one major assumption: that the sports industry will continue to be popular in the future. It's time to call that premise into question.

Don't worry - sports as a whole are not going to die out. However, the industry itself could be in danger of losing popularity when forced to take on its greatest threat: choice.

Entertainment is a zero-sum game. Whenever you choose to watch a certain show, there's another show that you're choosing not to watch. There is a limited amount of time each person can spend consuming content. With so many options available, will we really continue to rely on content that is only interesting when viewed live at a scheduled time and features an inconsistent product?

That's sports in a nutshell. You have to watch it when it happens, or it becomes old news. However, there's no guarantee the game will be good. It could be a blowout. Players and teams could perform poorly. Why would we waste our time on the unknown?

For the last century, sports have thrived because they provide reliable programming. We always knew when the game would be on, and we made sure to tune into it. Sports were and continue to be appointment television. Who would have thought this glorified attribute could eventually be its downfall?

Streaming services like Netflix and video-sharing platforms such as YouTube provide massive amounts of content that can be viewed at any time. You can binge-watch an entire season of a show in one day if you want to. Sporting events take place whether you're there watching or not. Accessibility is the future - the content comes to you, whenever you're ready.

Could we see the rise of scripted sports, made specifically for the digital world? With the outcomes knowing predetermined, the need to watch live wouldn't be as strong, but the excitement could be maintained. If an NFL season was told in the form of a Netflix series, could we script a better story than real life can provide? Television is better at crafting narratives and controlling audience reaction than sports, and in this scenario, there is no risk of injury to human athletes. After all, the competition isn't real.

To avoid this outcome and continue to thrive, there are important steps the sports world needs to take. Primarily, increasing access to sports, particularly at the youth level, must be made a priority. Additionally, our current sports must adapt to the digital age through changes in rules and presentation while we also work to push new sports into the mainstream and embrace trends such as esports. Lastly, it is essential that measures are taken to maintain competitive integrity and keep our sports safe, in order to create a positive environment.

The world is changing. Will sports be ready?

II: AN OVERINDULGENCE OF MADNESS

Originally published: April 11, 2019

Raining Takes
September 5, 2047

An Overindulgence of Madness
By Asher Raines

Underdog Stories

April 28, 4:30 a.m. - Wooden Complex, Court 73

Legends often arise out of the most unlikely circumstances. For Tanner Crowley, the present situation would certainly qualify. Just weeks before his graduation, the senior accounting major double-knotted his shoes and took the court to make his college basketball debut.

Fist-bumping seven-footer and future NBA lottery pick Rashaun Tate, Crowley couldn't help but marvel at the fulfillment of a lifelong goal - an opportunity that wouldn't have been possible before this year. It was nothing short of a dream. And yet, despite the ungodly hour, Tanner was wide awake. More than that, he was starting for Duke with a spot in the Sweet Sixteen on the line.

A strong performance and a victory would leave Crowley a hero, someone who would be talked about for years to come. But there was no time to think about that right now. There was only time for basketball.

The #2 seed Blue Devils were set to face off against the #39 seed Blazers of Valdosta State, who were looking to continue their miracle run following an upset of #7 seed Memphis approximately 17 minutes prior. That's a sentence I never thought I'd write.

What an intriguing matchup. On one side, there was Crowley, finally getting his chance to play for one of college basketball's historic programs. On the other side, a team new to Division I ball that had already made it further than anyone had anticipated and were now presented with the task of taking down that historic program. An underdog versus a team of underdogs. It's no surprise this was TV's featured game of the week.

There's an unshakeable appeal to the underdog story, and TV knows this better than anyone. Perhaps we see ourselves in the guy no one believed in and want to believe that in a world driven by elites, with hard work, determination, and maybe a bit of good fortune, anything is possible. That in our everyday lives, dreams can come true.

For someone, that dream was about to end.

I should have been eager to watch the game. The storyline was awfully compelling. Yet, because of the circumstances that led up to and surrounded this moment, I felt conflicted.

When I was born, March Madness had 68 teams. There were no gimmicks and qualifying for it still meant something. Unfortunately, the remnants of that old tournament are little more than dust in the wind. Today, we have two tournaments. One is a bloated, 128-team version of March Madness. The other is a new tournament, beginning just this year. It is the ultimate gimmick - a dangerous, convoluted mess of a game I love. A de-evolution of sport driven by capitalistic greed and serialized for the world to see. The one-day, 368-team "Summer Madness".

Consumption of a Rival

The downfall of order is marked by the perpetuation of innocent changes. Make enough alterations to a system, and slowly it will become unrecognizable. In this case, that process took over 100 years.

When Oregon defeated Ohio State to become champions of the inaugural NCAA Basketball Tournament in 1939, it was actually the separately organized National Invitational Tournament, or NIT, that was seen as the more prestigious tournament.

Predating the NCAA-sponsored event which would become March Madness by a year, the NIT's focus on gathering the best teams regardless of region and the media attention of playing at Madison Square Garden in New York City made it a more desired invitation for many schools. Notably, in 1944, DePaul turned down an offer to play in the NCAA Tournament, ultimately finishing as runner-up in the NIT.

However, there was no explicit rule against playing in both tournaments. That same year, Utah became the first team to do so after a tragic car accident left an Arkansas coaching aide dead and two players seriously injured, forcing the Razorbacks to drop out of the tournament and the NCAA to look for a replacement. That Utah team, which had fallen to Kentucky in the NIT quarterfinals, went on to win the NCAA Tournament and defeat eventual NIT winner St. John's in a charity game.

In 1950, The City College of New York (CCNY), won both tournaments, defeating Bradley in the finals of each. The following year, the NCAA made their first major move to seize control of postseason play by doubling their field to 16 teams, creating the first automatic berths for 10 conference champions, and requiring those conference champions to play in the tournament.

While the 1951 rules essentially forced many of the nation's best teams to play in the NCAA Tournament, it did not prohibit them from also competing in the NIT. That changed in 1953, when the NCAA expanded once again, this time to 22 teams, and ruled that teams could only participate in one postseason tournament. With a limited pool of teams to choose from, the NIT took a back seat to the NCAA Tournament, and never regained equal footing.

That's not to say teams never turned down NCAA bids for the NIT. In 1968, Bob Knight's Army team rejected a tournament bid in favor of the NIT, which Knight thought they had a better chance of winning. Knight and the Black Knights fell to Notre

Dame in the first round, and Army had to wait until 2024 to make their first March Madness appearance in school history.

As late as 1970, Marquette coach Al McGuire chose the NIT in protest of his team's placement in the Midwest Regional rather than the Mideast Regional closer to home. Luckily for McGuire, his team had more luck than the Army team of two years prior and won the NIT.

There would be no repeat performances by future teams looking to play in an easier or more local tournament, though. In 1971, the NCAA further hammered the nail in the NIT's coffin by preventing teams selected for the NCAA Tournament from playing in other postseason tournaments.

In 1975, the NCAA Tournament again expanded to 32 teams and began allowing each conference to receive one additional at-large bid, which had previously been restricted to independents. By 1980, the tournament had reached 48 teams and allowed conferences an unlimited number of at-large bids. Any team the NCAA wanted in its tournament played in its tournament. So much for the NIT.

Over time, the National Invitational Tournament became known by a plethora of other names, including the Not Important Tournament and the Not In Tournament. The NCAA eventually purchased the NIT in 2005, completing the consumption of its original rival.

Intentional Foul Play

April 27, 11:00 p.m. - Wooden Complex, Court 18

Kansas coach Austin Ratliff came to a realization. His team entered Summer Madness as tournament favorites - they were just weeks removed from a 37-4 season capped off with a National Championship. The Jayhawks, along with 143 other teams, would receive a first-round bye, but that still meant they would have to win eight games in less than a day's time to capture both titles.

This whole tournament was designed to induce chaos - how do you prepare for something like that? Surely, there would be no way to guarantee victory. In the real tournament, the favorites are no more than what - 15, 20 percent at winning the whole thing? There are a million more variables here. Finding any ways to control the randomness would be valuable.

One way to do just that would be to extend the tournament as long as possible. Since his team had the best roster in the country, Ratliff figured that any additional rest he could get his main rotation would increase their overall championship odds.

Creating that rest just required making use of some of the new rules implemented for the one-day, 368-team tournament. Namely, those stating that any student of a university with eligibility can play for that university and that players do not foul out at five fouls but are instead given fifteen fouls for the duration of the tournament.

In context, both of these rules make sense. Summer Madness is a marathon, not a sprint. There's almost no way a team could make it through the whole thing with just their normal roster, so they're allowed to bring extra manpower as they see fit. Kansas wasn't looking to play it close - they brought an extra 30 reserve players - more than any other school, giving them 45 total bodies to use at their discretion.

Giving players 15 fouls each was designed to add an extra strategic element to the affair. Players can stay in the game past the normal five-foul limit, but they risk limiting their availability for future games. As a coach, do you even play your stars in early games at all?

For Coach Ratliff, the answer to that question was easy, at least in terms of their second-round matchup against Jacksonville State. The opposing Gamecocks, who would've been at least 20-

point underdogs under normal circumstances, had just come out of a tight 64 vs. 65-seed matchup, prevailing against Bryant by just a bucket. They were exhausted, and after making the half-mile trek from Court 107 to Court 18, arrived for their matchup with the National Champions just six minutes before tip-off.

Kansas leaned heavily on their subs and reserves yet were still able to open up a substantial 64-35 lead by the end of the third quarter. Then, in the fourth, Coach Ratliff put his plan into motion. Five of his 30 extra players took the court and proceeded to intentionally foul five times, sending Jacksonville State into the bonus.

When they got the ball, the "Jayhawks" took the first good look they could create, and immediately went back to intentionally fouling. Over and over, this repeated for the entire 10-minute period. Jack Yarbrough fouled out of the game with two points and fifteen personal fouls in seven minutes of action. Even some of the Jacksonville State players got in on the intentional foul fun. The fourth quarter lasted an entire hour. At its conclusion, Kansas had prevailed 102-91.

Once the AMCA realized Kansas' plan, they quickly changed the rules, banning intentional fouling in future rounds by the leading team for what the referees deemed stalling. It may have only been good for one use, but the intentional foul strategy worked like a charm.

Spindletop

By 1985, the NCAA Tournament had expanded to 64 teams and adopted the moniker of March Madness. It was a period of time that modernized the sport of basketball. In terms of rules, 1985 saw the introduction of a shot clock, and the NCAA officially added the three-point line the following year, although some conferences had used it as early as the 1980-81 season.

As more regular season and tournament games were shown on TV, fan interest in the sport grew. Unlikely National Championship winners like Jim Valvano's 1983 NC State team, a #6 seed, and Rollie Massimino's 1985 Villanova Wildcats, who as a #8, are still the highest-seeded national champions to date, helped popularize the Cinderella story, and the notion that anyone could win the tournament. College basketball certainly wasn't the same as it had been in the 60s and 70s when John Wooden and UCLA won 10 titles over a span of 12 years.

An expanded 64-team field provided more opportunities for upsets that created excitement. Being a power of two, it also meant there was a clean-looking tournament bracket with no byes or play-in games, which made filling out a bracket much more appealing from a fan perspective.

The proliferation of bracket pools is what really turned March Madness into a cultural phenomenon. Tens of millions of people, even those who weren't fans of the sport and didn't pay attention to the regular season, started filling out brackets annually - competing with friends, family, and coworkers.

And not just competing - betting. Billions of dollars would be wagered every year on the tournament. That interest led to exponential growth in broadcast deals between the NCAA and TV networks, and massive advertising and sponsorship revenues. March Madness had everyone seeing green, becoming the NCAA's dominant source of revenue and the biggest annual sporting event in the United States.

The power to completely captivate a country for a few weeks a year. All from one 64-team tournament. A true pinnacle of sport, from the players, leaving it all out on the line for their One Shining Moment, to the coaches, school bands, and broadcasters. The excitement was unparalleled. The tournament was perfect. All the NCAA had to do was not change it.

Alas, nothing gold can stay.

Winning's Lament

The founding of the Mountain West Conference was the first domino. In its inaugural season of play in 2000, the new eight-team league formed by parting members of the Western Athletic Conference did not receive an automatic bid to the NCAA Tournament. The NCAA did not want to eliminate an at-large bid to make room for the 31st conference. To solve this dilemma, the NCAA decided the following year to expand March Madness to 65 teams, creating a play-in game for the two lowest-ranked teams to earn their spot in the Round of 64.

Outside of denying one #16 seed each year from a chance at taking down a #1, the move to 65 teams changed essentially nothing about the tournament. An innocent change, one might say. However, it did set the precedent that play-in games and expansion beyond 64 teams were okay.

Ten years later, the tournament would grow once more, to 68 teams. Another innocent change. The newly branded "First Four" in Dayton would pit the bottom four auto-bid teams against each other for the final two #16 seeds, while the last four at-larges in the field battled for what were usually #11 seeds. Adding a few extra at-large teams made it a little easier to make the tournament, but outside of talk of a "weak bubble," March Madness looked basically the same, and only continued to become more popular.

Just as with the 65-team field, things continued for some time. But by the start of the 2020s, expansion was on the NCAA's mind once again. Division I basketball had kept growing, now to over 350 schools, compared to just 282 in 1985, the start of the 64-team era. As many would note, for the same proportion of teams to make the tournament as did back then, the modern field would need to climb to 80.

The first official movement to expand beyond 68 came from the ACC in 2018, which proposed a 72-team tournament. Over the next few years, most conferences recommended the change - power conferences saw an opportunity to get more money from having more teams in the Big Dance, while mid-majors just wanted a better shot at an at-large berth.

In 2022, the NCAA made the change, adding four more at-large teams, and creating a second site in Salt Lake City to host the other half of the "Initial Eight" games alongside Dayton. Then in 2025, Buffalo and Oklahoma City joined the mix, and each site had its own First Four. Proportionality to 1985 had been achieved with an 80-team field.

But by now, the cracks in the format had shown themselves. With the 72-team field came the first .500 team to ever receive an at-large bid. Then, in 2027, under the 80-team format, a 16-17 Oklahoma team got in despite a losing record. It was a decision that seemed to go against the fundamental belief that winning was important. Advanced metrics shouldn't mean everything, but at some point, you just run out of better teams.

The admittedly impressive success rates of First Four teams in the Round of 64 was used to justify the addition of more play-in games, but this logic was always flawed. Upsets will always happen, no matter how teams are in the tournament. Even the worst team in the nation would pull out a victory eventually. Just because a team wins a March Madness game doesn't mean they deserved a spot in the field.

Once it was time to renew the March Madness television deals in 2033, the tournament hit its biggest growth spurt yet. 96 teams had been on the table, but the NCAA instead decided to go the whole nine yards, creating the 128-team field still in use for the main tourney today.

32 conference regular season champions, 32 conference tour-

nament champions, and 64 at-large selections comprise the monolithic event. An extra week had to be added just to play out all 64 opening-round matchups. Certainly, no one deserving would ever miss out on the fun again.

But is this even fun? For one thing, the 128-team field killed bracketology. People used to try to predict which teams would make March Madness, tracking projected seedings as the year went on. Now, it's largely pointless, as any team worth discussing is a shoo-in. Entire conferences get in and no one even blinks.

It feels like if you've beaten just about anyone, you can make it. Once upon a time, making the tournament was an accomplishment. Now, even the teams that were once considered "bad losses" are going dancing.

There was never a need to grow this big. It doesn't matter how many teams make the playoffs in pro sports leagues. It doesn't matter how many college football teams make bowl games. March Madness should contain as many teams as deserve to make it. 64 was that magic number. College football figured that out when they expanded to an eight-team field.

Modern March Madness is simply too much for most people to keep up with. The tourney lasts more than three weeks. Brackets can't even be printed or filled out on a standard sheet of paper. Good luck with trying to research every team. Maybe it's a dream come true for some hoop heads, but you won't convince me this has been a positive change.

Gone are the NIT, the CIT, and the CBI. How can any other tournament possibly compete, or even find teams worth inviting? What good is scraping the bottom of the barrel?

We could have returned to the glory days. When corruption scandals took down the NCAA, and the Association of Major Collegiate Athletics (AMCA) was formed to take its place, there were questions about if any changes would be made to postseason tournaments. I campaigned for a return to a 64-team March Madness. You know what happened instead.

Constructing the Absurd

Once something is financially stable, good luck making it smaller. Growth is just an extension of supply and demand. Take a look at any of the leagues that have started up and folded over the years. When things look good, they add teams. Then, when the tides turn, the league gets smaller, usually ceasing operations shortly thereafter.

March Madness, regardless of its issues, remains huge, so there were really only two options: keep it as is, or make it even bigger. The AMCA's conclusion pulled from both. Keep the 128-team field, but also create a separate tournament entirely, one where everyone gets a shot at the trophy.

The notion of a 368-team tournament is utterly ridiculous. But that's only where it starts. A 368-team tournament played entirely within 24 hours? That's unfathomable. It just doesn't seem possible from a travel perspective, logistics perspective, or physical limitations of the human body perspective. In no universe does this seem remotely safe or doable. But you can't just have another normal tournament. So, enter the behemoth.

For one weekend at the end of April, just before finals season, the basketball teams for all 368 AMCA Division I schools meet up in St. Louis, most arriving by Hyperloop. There they find the Wooden Complex, a basketball mecca years in the making, designed specifically to host the nonsense about to take place. In the center, an Olympic village of sorts houses the well over 10,000 players, coaches, and trainers for their stay. Surrounding the lodging are 150 basketball courts in 10 separate facilities, along with numerous restaurants, medical centers, and resting areas.

Friday night and Saturday morning are designated for the

media to conduct pre-tournament interviews, and then Saturday night, the marathon gets underway, running non-stop until only one team is left standing.

At 7 p.m., the opening round begins, with matchups to determine the final 112 spots in the Terrific Two Hundred Fifty-Six. I kid. Numbers that big do not deserve alliterative monikers. Simultaneously, all the locations for the second-round matchups are announced, allowing all the teams with first-round byes to make their way to warm-ups.

As a rule, locations for each round are announced once the preceding round begins, just to keep everyone on their toes. In the earlier rounds, unlucky teams could be forced to travel nearly a mile in between games, which could get dicey as once the final game of a round ends, there are only 15 minutes before all games of the next round begin. Any team that isn't ready to play at tip-time is immediately disqualified.

To cope with the physical toll of playing eight or nine games back-to-back, a rule was made to allow any student of a university with remaining eligibility to compete, allowing deeper-than-usual rosters. The AMCA also decided to experiment with the actual rules of the game, similar to how the NIT once did. Among the changes for the inaugural tournament were the rule giving players 15 fouls to use at any point during the tournament, the inclusion of a four-point line 30 feet away from the basket, and a 5-on-4 power play as a result of technical and flagrant fouls.

Why would teams decide to partake in this fiesta after the season has concluded? Partially because the AMCA says they have to. But really, like most things, it's about money. For each game a school wins, they earn a greater share of overall tournament revenues. The whole effort takes a ton of coordination and manpower, but once a year, everyone is more than happy to unite and embrace the occasion.

Ws, Ls, and Zs

April 28, 6:00 a.m. - Section 4 Rest Area

Notre Dame senior forward Dante Collins was in for a rude awakening in the literal sense. After leading a successful comeback in the fourth round that kept the Irish in the tournament but well exceeded his intended minutes restriction of 15 per game until the Final Four, the plan was to allow him to rest a game and return, at least somewhat recharged, for the Sweet Sixteen.

It was a roll of the dice - not necessarily a required course of action, but a forward-looking decision. The sort of gamble it takes to come out on top of a 368-team field. Unfortunately, it hadn't paid off. At halftime, Notre Dame found themselves down 15 points to Belmont. That's when a trainer was sent to put an early end to Collins' snooze and escort him straight to the court. But despite an impressive effort, Notre Dame failed to cheat death for the second straight game.

To say winning eight or nine games in just one day is grueling would be the ultimate understatement. The ideal scenario is to reach the championship game with your typical rotation fully rested and ready to go. Unfortunately, that isn't possible, which means teams with title aspirations need to come up with strategies to manage rotations and balance minutes played.

Each real contender attempted to do this in a different way. Some played their regular starters at the beginning of games, hoping to build an early lead before sending in the reserves. Some always tried to have at least one starter on the floor at all times. Others attempted to rest their starters entirely for the first couple of rounds.

Many teams made use of the designated rest areas to give players short breaks, especially when an outcome seemed to be decided early. Even a significant number of coaches made time for naps, as the energy required just to stay awake and mentally focused provided a major challenge. Teams utilized everything from energy drinks and coffee to meditation and yoga as ways to stay alert. Trainers worked overtime trying to make sure players stayed as limber as possible.

No matter the team, though, those who felt they had a chance to win it all shared a common philosophy of trying to preserve themselves - not go all out early on. But as these teams quickly learned, that would prove troublesome.

Naturally, we like to focus our attention on the power conferences and high-profile programs, especially when there is a dizzying number of schools to follow. However, that ignores hundreds of teams, most of which just aren't equipped to go the distance. They don't have the talent or the numbers to make it all the way. This holds especially true for schools with smaller student bodies, without the large pool of reserves to bring along.

For these teams, there is no "rest for later". Wins are money, and because they aren't supposed to go deep in the first place, they're all-in from the get-go. As a few top teams learned the hard way with stunning upset defeats, you can't just bank on getting by with guys you practically pulled off the street. The big names are going to have to play.

As the tournament goes on, opponents get tougher, fatigue sets in, and games become harder to win. You need your stars but are forced to rely on everyone else as well. It's impossible calculus. Let the science experiment begin. How many minutes can the human body handle? How long can one play basketball?

The Revolution Will Be Televised

In today's age, basketball is ubiquitous. The most popular sport in the nation, James Naismith's game can feel like the center of the universe sometimes. But why settle for sometimes when you can have all the time?

The AMCA didn't decide to create a second tournament just because. Nor would they be able to generate much revenue from a 24-hour event, much of which takes place while most people are asleep. No, it was made to fill a gap.

Collegiate athletics is held together by two sports: basketball and football. Football season starts late August or early September, with basketball picking up in the middle of football season and through early April.

But after that? Baseball does its best to carry the torch through its World Series in June, but July and August present a dead zone while students are on Summer break. And without the playoffs of any major professional sports going on either, that's time for the taking, and an opportunity the AMCA looked to seize.

The tournament might be played during the last weekend of April, but it is not broadcast until July, hence the name "Summer Madness". For fans, Summer Madness takes place over eight weeks, one round per week with the Final Four combined into one.

Each week, the marquee matchups and best overall games are shown on television and streamed online, along with highlights and analysis shows. Special subscription packages allow every game to be seen in its entirety, along with exclusive team cameras following each school for every minute of the tournament, even conducting interviews during the move between games. Talk shows discuss the events and storylines as if they just happened because it's the first time anyone who wasn't there has seen it.

During the playing of the tournament, security is extremely tight. The only people allowed in each arena are the teams, referees, camera crews, scoreboard operators, and the small media team assigned to each school. No fans, bands, or cheerleaders.

No commentators - they see it when the rest of the world does.

As the tournament progresses, eliminated teams and everyone working at gyms which are no longer in use are quickly filed out of the Wooden Complex and forbidden to discuss what they've seen in order to preserve gambling markets, which predictably go out of control.

Months-old footage presented, watched, discussed, debated, and bet on as if it was happening live. A blending of reality commanding hefty rights fees and lucrative sponsorships. The future in the form of the past brought to life – just another unique aspect of the most idiosyncratic competition to hit the mainstream.

Fifteen Minutes / Empty Gyms

A 368-team tournament requires 367 losers. You'd be hard-pressed to find another event that crushes dreams at such a ludicrous rate. However, few also create so much hope. Nowhere is that hope stronger than in those who aren't student-athletes at all, the more than 2,000 players who were added to their school's rosters specifically for Summer Madness. Single elimination takes on a whole new meaning when this tournament is the only chance you'll ever have to play collegiate basketball.

Remember Tanner Crowley from earlier? He was the Duke senior making his first appearance in the Round of 32 against Valdosta State. Crowley was an intramural champion - a scrappy player and tenacious defender from the point guard position; a real hustle and heart guy. He could run for days, a particularly valuable skill in this tournament.

Suiting up for the Blue Devils allowed him a chance at greatness. To be, if only for a moment, the player he always thought he would become. So, what happened? Crowley played the first five minutes of the game, missed his only shot, and then returned to the bench, where he spent his team's first three games, to watch

Duke become another upset victim. Tanner Crowley's college basketball career ended nearly as quickly as it started, a blip in the history books of a game Duke fans would want to forget.

This is the reality of Summer Madness. Despite how stories are cherry-picked to try and convince us otherwise, most reserves will not do anything of significance. The majority will never even set foot on the court. They never get their fifteen minutes of fame. Instead, all that awaits them is a lonely transportation back to their normal lives.

Perhaps knowledge of how rare success is, especially for a reserve, makes it all the sweeter. When Valdosta State knocked off Duke, they did so with heavy contributions from reserves, including an unbelievable team-high 24 points from Quentin Murphy, whose first career action had come in the game before. Murphy's outburst came practically out of nowhere and turned him into a sensation for the week after the game officially aired.

There are two sides to every coin, though, and the Cinderella run of Summer Madness 2047 reached a painful conclusion two hours later in the Sweet Sixteen when Murphy's game-winning three-point attempt against Michigan rimmed out. Heartbroken and exhausted from another herculean effort, Murphy passed out on the hardwood, his body a portrait of fruitless exertion.

At least Murphy had his moment. What he and that Valdosta State team accomplished was nothing short of incredible, but I imagine it'll be soon forgotten as well. Inflation of tournament size brings opportunities but makes it harder for any specific team to be remembered when similar stories are bound to happen most years.

History remembers the victors. Not so much everyone who had to fall for them to claim the throne. For every dream that continues in a tournament like Summer Madness, another must meet its demise. But eventually, nearly everyone is the unlucky one, and shattered hopes haunt the empty gyms left behind.

Pyrrhic Victory

April 28, 3:50 p.m. - Wooden Complex, Court 1

Nearly 21 hours and 366 games after it began, what remained of the Michigan Wolverines and Central Florida Knights basketball teams took the court for one final clash to decide the fate of the inaugural Summer Madness tournament. The path had not been pretty - both teams had sustained injuries to key players and narrowly avoided defeat on their collision course with destiny. Across the tournament, especially in the later rounds, injuries had occurred at a tremendous rate.

There was no time for advanced scouting reports; there never had been. Even if some assistant coach had managed to put together a game plan, I'm not sure anyone would have been alert enough to follow it. Some players had fallen asleep. Others' bodies were shutting down, like Michigan's Justin Simmons, who by this point had been awake for 30 hours straight and played 154 total minutes, the equivalent of nearly four entire games. Nothing was left in the tank. Even those who had played very little struggled to stay energized.

Still, both teams were able to field five-man squads, fueled by caffeine and playing on instinct. The game was competitive, although the quality left something to be desired. It played out something like one of those "so bad it's good" movies. Mandatory viewing of a different sort. You couldn't blame the players, though. Everyone was giving their all; there just wasn't much all to give.

At 5:42 p.m., the final buzzer sounded. By a score of 57-52, UCF had emerged victorious as the first champions of Summer Madness. Reactions were a mixture of joy and relief. There would be no celebration that night. Only sleep.

An Overindulgence of Madness

The AMCA got their wish – a 368-team college basketball tournament played over the span of one day. It ran as smoothly as they could've hoped and became a massive commercial success. But at what cost?

To me, Summer Madness felt almost like a scam. The tournament itself isn't scripted, but the way it was created - entirely for money and ratings - made everything seem hollow and fake.

In a way, it might be our fault. The AMCA knew that if they created a second tournament, even with the most ridiculous premise imaginable, we wouldn't be able to get enough of it. As humans, we are never fully pleased. Everything good must become bigger, better, crazier. That mindset can lead to innovation, but also a perpetual state of dissatisfaction. In today's age, more content has only made us less content.

So, we tune in every week to watch as young men push themselves beyond their limits, to the point of exhaustion and injury, for an arbitrary title. Summer Madness is the Hunger Games, and we are citizens of the capitol. When players go too far and end up hurt, we are partially responsible for supporting the machine.

Yet, to do otherwise would be to deny every single participant a chance at a dream. The athletes are all good people, just being taken advantage of by the system. When combating corruption means crushing dreams, what are we supposed to do?

This story is not just about basketball - it is about consumerism, excess, and the guilty feeling of overindulgence. The 64-team March Madness was perfect. At 128 teams, it is heavily flawed but still manageable. Summer Madness is the extra bite that makes you sick.

I can't help but wonder what John Wooden would think. The venue for Summer Madness was named for the legendary UCLA coach, yet the tournament seems to go against everything

Wooden stood for.

After all of this, what's next? When is the expansion to 512 teams? When do we bring in Division II and III schools? How about international teams? It's only a matter of time before talks start on the next big thing. Sometimes I wonder if we could have been warned. But what's the point? No one would have listened.

III: OUT OF THE DAWG HOUSE: THE STORY OF THE 2018 CLEVELAND BROWNS

Originally published: August 3, 2019

Judgment Day

December 30, 2019

It's a situation that has to be seen — or heard, rather — to be believed. On the final day of the NFL regular season, an entire stadium of fans is chanting "LET'S GO BROWNS!" The moment is remarkable for a couple of reasons. For one, the Cleveland Browns are doing something meaningful during Week 17. That almost never happens. But the more astonishing element is where the chant is occurring.

This isn't Cleveland.

A stadium-wide Browns cheer is taking place in Heinz Field, home of the Pittsburgh Steelers, an AFC North rival of the Browns. On almost any other day, Pittsburgh would be rooting against the Browns. But at this moment, the Steelers' playoff hopes lie in the hands of Browns quarterback Baker Mayfield.

Entering this last Sunday of action, the 8–6–1 Steelers needed a win and help to keep their season alive. Trailing by half a game in the division to the 9–6 Baltimore Ravens and assuming no ties take place, Pittsburgh required a victory over the Cincinnati Bengals plus a Browns victory against the Ravens to avoid an early offseason.

Steelers star wide receiver Antonio Brown would be prepared to cheer for Cleveland. On the Wednesday before the games, he tweeted a picture of three of his own jerseys, modified with the letter S taped onto the end of the names, turning them from Brown jerseys to Browns jerseys.

On Sunday, the first half of the Steelers plan, while rocky at best, ultimately went as intended. Despite playing without Brown and trailing 10–0 late in the first half, the Steelers managed to tie things up in the third quarter before winning 16–13 on a late field goal by kicker Matt McCrane, who had been signed just two days earlier.

Meanwhile, things weren't going as well for the Browns. After trailing the Ravens 20–7 at halftime, Cleveland was mounting a comeback, but still trailed 26–24 after scoring a touchdown with 3:24 left in the fourth quarter.

However, after forcing a three-and-out, the Browns got the ball back at their own 26-yard line with less than two minutes on the clock and one timeout left. Trailing by two points, a field goal would be enough to win the game.

The crowd at Heinz Field was acutely aware of this. Since the Steelers game finished first, the end of the Browns game was being displayed on the video screens inside the stadium. Steelers players stayed on the field, watching with their fans as their season hung in the balance.

Pittsburgh still had a shot. Unfortunately, it lay in the hands of the worst team in modern NFL history.

Over the last two decades, the Browns had been historically terrible. We're talking two winning seasons, one playoff appearance, zero division titles terrible. Over the previous two years, the Browns won just a single game. In 2017, the Browns became just the second team in NFL history to go 0–16.

With your season on the line, this is not the team you want to roll the dice with. But the Steelers had no choice — they needed to have faith in the Cleveland Browns, a franchise that specializes in disappointment.

Luckily, things were looking up for the Browns in 2018. Just a year after going winless, Cleveland turned into one of the most exciting teams in the NFL, with a rollercoaster season that started with what I consider the most unpredictable seven weeks in NFL history.

By the time their Week 17 encounter with the Ravens came around, the Browns were 7–7–1 and playing to secure their first winning season since 2007.

Understanding the importance of this game and this season requires taking a deep dive into the history of a franchise that started out dominant before falling upon hard times, and later, total hopelessness. But sometimes, even for the hopeless, there is light at the end of the tunnel.

Riches to Rags

Let's go back — all the way back, to the founding of this franchise we've all come to associate with football futility.

In 1944, the All-America Football Conference was founded to rival the NFL following the end of World War II. When businessman Mickey McBride was awarded a franchise in Cleveland, his first move was to hire Paul Brown, a former National Championship-winning head coach at the high school and college levels, to coach the team. Brown was additionally given an ownership stake and control of player personnel. He became the team's namesake, and the Cleveland Browns were born.

When the AAFC began its play in 1946, so did the Browns. Led by coach Paul Brown and quarterback Otto Graham, the Browns were dominant, winning four straight AAFC championships, including an undefeated campaign in 1948.

Following the 1949 season, the AAFC folded. However, the Browns joined the NFL and kept winning, reaching the NFL Championship Game in each of the next six seasons, winning three titles.

To recap, in their first 10 seasons in franchise history, the Browns made their league championship game every year, collecting seven championships. It was regularly scheduled destruction on the gridiron, a near-perfect dismantling of foes.

Otto Graham retired after that seventh title, while Paul Brown stayed at the helm of the team he created through 1962. The team was still successful, largely due to the 1957 drafting of Jim Brown, but Cleveland failed to win a title during the period.

That, combined with some internal feuding, was enough for young owner Art Modell, who purchased the team for just shy of $4 million in 1961, to fire the only head coach in team history.

New coach Blanton Collier brought the Browns back to their championship ways, with four championship appearances in his tenure from 1963–70, including a title in 1964.

But that 1964 victory would be the Browns' last to date. They have never won a Super Bowl. They have never even appeared in one.

In 24 seasons, the Browns had reached 15 championships, winning eight of them. They finished under .500 just once. Those numbers were unmatched over that time span, making the Cleveland Browns arguably the most dominant professional football team prior to the NFL/AFL merger. And after that, nothing.

Once the 70s hit, the Browns turned into an unremarkable, run of the mill franchise. Some years were good, but most were pretty average, if not worse.

In 1990, now more than a quarter-century after their last championship, things hit rock bottom in Cleveland. The team finished 3–13, marking the worst record in franchise history. That year, the Browns allowed 462 points, more than any other team in the entire 1990s.

The abysmal season prompted Modell, who remained the owner of the team, to nearly completely overhaul the coaching staff, including signing a new head coach and defensive coordinator. Their names were Bill Belichick and Nick Saban.

Perhaps you've heard of them.

Since 2000, Bill Belichick has been the head coach of the New

England Patriots, where he has won six Super Bowls, more than any coach in NFL history, and led the greatest dynasty post-merger.

Meanwhile, Nick Saban has won six college football National Championships between his time at LSU and Alabama. The two are widely considered to be the best NFL and college head coaches in the modern era.

But even these two football geniuses, and friends, now with a dozen titles between them, couldn't bring back the glory days in Cleveland. In their four seasons together, 1991–94, the Browns had a regular-season record of 31–33 with just one play-off appearance. Nick Saban would refer to the period as the worst years of his life.

Following the 1994 season, Saban left the team to become the head coach at Michigan State. Belichick would stay one year longer, going 5–11 in 1995 before being fired by Modell.

During that season, the Browns' 50th overall, Modell announced his intention to move the Browns from Cleveland to Baltimore, citing a lack of both funds and will from the city of Cleveland to build a world-class stadium.

Following a lawsuit by the city of Cleveland, a settlement was reached that allowed Modell to move the team but guaranteed that football would return to the city in 1999, along with a new stadium.

Officially, the Browns name was "deactivated" for three years, while the team owned by Art Modell was reborn as the Baltimore Ravens.

The Curse

When the original Browns left Cleveland, they did not do so without repercussions. For a franchise with such remarkable beginnings, they had become entirely irrelevant. Even with two men who would become the greatest coaches of their era, the franchise squandered an opportunity to get back on track. Then, they simply moved away, leaving their history behind to start anew.

This angered the football gods. When the time came in 1999 for a new team to bear the same name, the gods began to exact their cruel revenge.

The Cleveland Browns are cursed. Since their 1999 return and leading into the 2018 season, the Browns had completed 19 of the most hopeless seasons in the history of professional sports.

Over this span, the new Browns had won just under 29% of their games, with an all-time record of just 88–216. It's normal for an expansion team to struggle in their first few years before gradually joining the rest of the pack. The Browns had done the opposite. In their most recent 10 seasons, they were just 38–122, for a winning percentage of 23.75%. Over time, the Browns were only getting worse.

The statistics to describe the Browns' futility are never-ending. Through 19 seasons, they made the playoffs just once (a first-round exit in 2002), finished with a winning record just twice, and won five or fewer games 14 times. In 15 of 19 campaigns, the Browns finished last in their division.

For comparison, during the same period, the Ravens made the playoffs 10 times and won two Super Bowls. Of course, neither iteration of the Browns has even played in a Super Bowl. From 1999–2017, the Browns finished with a better record than the Ravens just twice. Head-to-head, the Ravens led the series 29–9. Since the teams were both in the AFC North, the Ravens got to play Cleveland two times a year. For the Browns, it was a twice-annual reminder of what could have been.

Perhaps Art Modell was a visionary who knew he needed to get out of Cleveland at all costs. Either way, the Ravens became an

NFL success story while the city they left behind continued to suffer.

In their first 19 seasons, the Browns started 29 different quarterbacks, unable to find sustained success with any of them. In fact, the winningest quarterback at FirstEnergy Stadium in Cleveland isn't a Brown at all — it's Ben Roethlisberger of the Steelers! Despite not being drafted until 2004 and only getting to play in Cleveland once a year, he has 11 road wins over the Browns, more than any Browns QB has at their home stadium.

Losing leads to top draft picks, but for Cleveland, the NFL Draft has been a continuous disaster, one bust after the next.

They had a chance at Tom Brady. Back in the sixth round of the 2000 NFL Draft, the Browns were thinking quarterback. However, they decided on Spergon Wynn, who lasted just one year for the Browns, starting a single game. 16 picks later, the Patriots selected Brady, and their league domination commenced soon after.

The Browns have been victorious in a Week 1 matchup just once. In 2008, they went the final six games of the season without scoring an offensive touchdown.

However, none of this compares to what the Browns accomplished in 2016 and 2017, the first two seasons under the tenure of the team's ninth head coach, Hue Jackson. In 2016, the Browns nearly went winless, picking up their first and only victory of the season against the Chargers in Week 16, on Christmas Eve. An early present, indeed.

In 2017, the Browns one-upped themselves, losing six one-score games, including twice in overtime, on their way to the second 0–16 season in NFL history.

Things were looking up for the team after drafting defensive end Myles Garrett #1 overall, and also grabbing safety Jabrill Peppers and tight end David Njoku in the first round. They even went a perfect 4–0 in the preseason.

But the winning ended there. DeShone Kizer, a second-round draft pick and the newest in a line of Browns quarterback hopefuls, had a disastrous rookie campaign, starting 15 games and completing just over half his passes to go with 11 touchdowns and a league-leading 22 interceptions. The team would finish that season with a -28 turnover differential, the worst margin in the Super Bowl era.

There was some bad luck involved, though. Legendary offensive tackle Joe Thomas, who had never missed a snap in his career while making the Pro Bowl in each of his first 10 seasons, suffered a torn triceps in Week 7. It would be the final play of Thomas' career.

In Week 17 against the Steelers, the Browns had one final chance to avoid going winless. Down 28–24 with less than two minutes to play, Cleveland faced fourth and two from the Pittsburgh 27. Kizer avoided the sack, scrambling and finding an open Corey Coleman on the left sideline near the 11-yard line. The pass was on point. The ball went through Coleman's hands — incomplete.

The Cleveland Browns never had possession of the ball again. 0–16. Any Browns fan that thought it couldn't get any worse back in 1990 or 1995 had now endured 19 years of constant disasters, capped off with a zero-win season.

By the end of 2017, Cleveland was no longer located in Ohio; it resided at the bottom of the Mariana Trench.

Turning Tides?

At least in part, the Browns' ineptitude on the football field had been masked by the success of basketball in the city. Led by LeBron James, the Cleveland Cavaliers made the NBA Finals four consecutive seasons from 2014–15 to 2017–18. By winning the title in 2016, the Cavs snapped an over half-century title drought in Cleveland dating back to the Browns' last champion-ship in 1964.

If the Cavaliers allowed the Browns to escape responsibility for their failures, there would no longer be a place to hide. On July 1, 2018, LeBron agreed to a four-year, $154 million contract with the Los Angeles Lakers. It was a move that crippled the Cavaliers (they would go 19–63 the following season) and left the city of Cleveland without a star.

On the football side of things, the only point of stability over the last decade had been at left tackle, where Joe Thomas had played 10,363 consecutive snaps across 167 games. Thomas was now retired. This offseason would be critical, as the Browns needed to find a face for their franchise and keep fans interested in the team.

General manager John Dorsey and the Browns would make the most of their offseason moves before LeBron's announcement, but to their credit, they knew they needed to get to work.

DeShone Kizer was not the quarterback of the future. So, they sent him to Green Bay for corner Demarious Randall. In his place, they got three-year Bills starter Tyrod Taylor for their third-round pick. Then, they called up the Dolphins and picked up Pro Bowl wide receiver Jarvis Landry for a 2018 fourth-rounder and a seventh in 2019. When former 49ers running back Carlos Hyde signed with the Browns in free agency, it seemed to complete a new-look offense for the team.

But they weren't done yet. In fact, the team's biggest moves came from the draft. Once again with the #1 overall pick, Cleveland selected Oklahoma's Heisman Trophy-winning quar-terback Baker Mayfield. Mayfield was a somewhat controversial player in college, and in a QB-heavy draft, many thought USC's Sam Darnold would be the first man off the board.

Still, Mayfield was a leader — a passionate, high energy guy that could play. While he wouldn't be slated to start immediately, this was a guy for fans to be excited about. A guy that could become the face of a franchise the Browns so desperately desired.

With the fourth overall pick, the Browns selected cornerback Denzel Ward. Early in the second round, they took running back Nick Chubb. It appeared to be a strong draft for Cleveland, but little did anyone know, Mayfield, Ward, and Chubb would exceed all expectations in their rookie seasons.

The Browns were gaining momentum and had the opportunity to showcase it to the world by appearing on HBO's Hard Knocks, where the Browns got even stronger with the news that oft-suspended wide receiver Josh Gordon would be hopeful to be ready to play in Week 1.

After going 1–31 in his first two seasons at the position (the worst two-year stretch in NFL history), the pressure was on head coach Hue Jackson to translate all the new talent at his disposal into wins.

Many were surprised to see Jackson return for a third year. Among those was probably Jackson himself. In his only prior head coaching gig, the Raiders fired Jackson after a single 8–8 season in 2011. The Browns were certainly giving him a longer leash.

It's hard to make judgments before the regular season, but entering 2018, the Browns looked like a different team — literally. Of the 53 players on the 2017 Browns Week 17 roster, only 19 remained by Week 1 of 2018. That's an incredible amount of turnover. Many of the players that did stick around were part of a defense that was actually decent, finishing 14th in yards allowed per game the year prior.

With all their new signings, draft picks, and existing young talent, the Browns became a trendy surprise playoff pick despite having an over-under win total set at 5.5, joint-lowest in the league with the Arizona Cardinals.

Fans clung to the storyline of the lovable losers finally looking competitive, and Bud Light hopped on board too, introducing the "Victory Fridges," chain locked refrigerators of Bud Light in Cleveland bars, only to be opened when the Browns won their first game of the season.

Browns players only added to the hype. Tyrod Taylor predicted that Cleveland would "shock the world", while Jarvis Landry said the team had potential to win the Super Bowl and score 40 points per game.

For a team coming off just the second 0–16 season in NFL history, the Cleveland Browns entered 2018 with the swagger of a Super Bowl contender. There was just one thing left to do — prove it. With Week 1 looming, the new-look Browns would finally get that chance.

The Rollercoaster

Earlier, I mentioned that the 2018 Browns started their season with the most unpredictable seven weeks in NFL history. To show you what I mean, let's take it one week at a time.

Week 1: Browns vs. Steelers

In a game where the Steelers turn the ball over six times, the Browns find themselves trailing 21–7 in the fourth quarter. It's not a promising opening for the revamped offense, led by Tyrod Taylor, the 29th Browns starting QB in 20 seasons. They do manage to tie things up at 21 all, though, when Taylor connects with Josh Gordon on a 17-yard touchdown at the two-minute warning.

And following a Pittsburgh three-and-out, the Browns get the ball back with a chance to win it in regulation. Unfortunately, facing 1st-and-10 at the Steelers' 43 with 23 seconds left, Taylor throws a pick. Overtime.

The extra period starts with a Browns punt, followed by a Steelers punt, and another Browns punt. Finally, the Steelers have a drive going, needing only a field goal to win the game. Chris Boswell gets a shot from 42 yards out but puts it wide left. The Browns are still in this one but will go a third straight overtime drive without picking up a first down, sending things back to Ben Roethlisberger.

It's Steelers ball, looking to make something happen in the game's final plays. Instead, the Browns get a strip-sack and return the fumble to the Steelers' 12...almost. Myles Garrett gets called for an illegal block on the return, sending the ball back to the 24 with 36 seconds left. After a run loses a yard, Browns kicker Zane Gonzales trots out for a 43-yarder.

Once again, a field goal for the win. But this kick doesn't even get a chance. It's blocked by T.J. Watt, and the game ends in a tie.

Let the jokes roll in. The Browns managed to snap a 17-game losing streak without winning. They also managed to tie their average win total from the past two seasons with half a win. Hey, at least it's already better than last year!

The game was statistically remarkable for the Browns' inability to win with a +5 turnover differential. As Bill Barnwell later pointed out, since the Browns returned in 1999, teams with a +5 or better turnover differential had gone 132–4–1. After Week 1, the Browns accounted for two of those losses and the tie. Rest of NFL: 130–2. Browns: 2–2–1.

To make matters worse, after the game, the NFL's head of officiating admitted that the refs blew a roughing the passer call on Myles Garrett in the second quarter which led to a Steelers touchdown on the very next play.

There were still some positives to be found, though. Denzel Ward had two interceptions in his first career game and would win the Pepsi Rookie of the Week award. Plus, a tie against the

Steelers isn't a bad result at all.

Still, what a way to way to start the season. And we're only getting started.

Week 2: Browns @ Saints

The Browns' quest to unlock the Bud Light fridges brought them to New Orleans, where, somehow, they managed to hold Drew Brees and the potent Saints offense to just a field goal through three quarters. Browns 12, Saints 3.

Alas, it wouldn't be that simple. Brees proceeded to throw two touchdowns to Michael Thomas. A two-point conversion gave the Saints an 18–12 lead with 2:40 left.

But the Browns strike quickly. With 1:16 remaining, Taylor hits Antonio Callaway for a 47-yard score. 18–18. With the PAT, Zane Gonzales can put the Browns back on top.

He misses.

It's his second missed extra point of the day to go along with a missed field goal. We're still tied.

On the second play of the following drive, Brees finds Ted Ginn Jr. for 42 yards to the Browns' 25. A few plays later, Wil Lutz connects on a field goal to give the Saints a 21–18 lead. Crucially though, the Browns still have 21 seconds to work with.

Miraculously, the Browns need just two plays to set up Gonzales with a 52-yard try to send the game into overtime. However, Gonzales misses his fourth kick of the game, and the Browns lose by three.

After the game, the team would cut Gonzales, who, unbeknownst to coach Hue Jackson, had been playing with a groin injury. In his place, the Browns signed undrafted rookie Greg Joseph.

They would also trade Josh Gordon to the Patriots. Gordon had missed the game with a hamstring injury sustained at a promotional shoot, marking a disappointing end to his tumultuous time in Cleveland.

Week 3: Browns vs. Jets

In what looked like a mistake on the part of the schedule makers, the Browns hosted the Jets in Week 3 on Thursday Night Football.

I kid.

It was an intended matchup between the top two quarterbacks taken in the 2018 NFL Draft: #1 pick Baker Mayfield and #3 pick Sam Darnold. The Browns weren't intending to play Mayfield, but after Tyrod Taylor, who had been struggling, suffered a concussion in the second quarter, Mayfield got his first taste of NFL action with the Browns down 14–0.

Mayfield's impact was immediate. In his first possession, he ran the two-minute drill effectively, leading to a Greg Joseph field goal before halftime. Joseph would add another field goal in the third quarter before Mayfield led his first touchdown drive, with Carlos Hyde punching in a one-yard score. The Browns ran some trickery on a two-point conversion, with Mayfield catching a pass from Jarvis Landry to knot things at 14.

After a long Jets drive resulted in a field goal, Mayfield led an equally long touchdown drive of nearly seven minutes, giving the Browns a 21–17 lead late, which they hold onto, following a pair of Darnold interceptions in the final two minutes.

Dilly Dilly, open the fridges! The Cleveland Browns have won a game of football! It's the team's first win in 635 days, since December of 2016. It also appeared to be a changing of the guard. Baker Mayfield stepped up and played a great game, going 17/23 for 201 yards in just over a half of action, leading a big comeback victory.

In front of the home fans, Mayfield's message came loud and clear: I'm not the future — I'm the right now. Mayfield had won the starting job and was set to become the Browns' 30th starting quarterback since 1999.

Week 4: Browns @ Raiders

As a reward for their first win in a football game in two years, the Browns got to play in a baseball stadium. No, seriously — the Oakland Raiders play in a baseball stadium. There's a lot to tackle here, so I'll move quickly.

Baker Mayfield throws an early pick-six, but the Browns respond with 28 of the game's next 35 points to take a 28–14 lead midway through the third quarter. Over the next 12 minutes of game time, the Raiders scored 20 points on four separate drives to go back up 34–28.

Not to be one-upped, the Browns scored touchdowns on consecutive series and led 42–34 with four minutes and 20 seconds left. Because of course they do. Talk about a back-and-forth affair. They could have scored even faster but a Derek Carr fumble which would've been returned for a touchdown by Larry Ogunjobi is blown dead early for forward progress, making the play non-reviewable. After the game, the league will once again admit they made a mistake.

Trailing by eight points, Derek Carr marches his team all the way down to first and ten at the Browns 11. They reach as close as the six-yard line but turn the ball over on downs.

No, we're not done yet.

The Browns fail to pick up a first down to seal the game. Carlos Hyde appears to do so on 3rd & 2. However, review overturns the play, forcing a punt.

And since this is how Browns games work, the Raiders score a touchdown in less than a minute and get the two-point conversion. 42–42. Mayfield is intercepted on a deep ball to put the Browns in chip-shot field goal range, and another game heads to overtime.

In OT, Raiders kicker Matt McCrane (yes, the same McCrane who would later kick for the Steelers in Week 17) misses a 50-yard field goal, giving the Browns good field position at their own 40. But just like overtime against the Steelers, the Browns can't get anything going. The Raiders get McCrane another chance from 29 yards out, and he converts.

It's a heartbreaker for the Browns — a game they absolutely should've won. Yet, the final score reads Raiders 45, Browns 42.

Bad news: the Browns are only 1–2–1. Good news: Nick Chubb broke off a pair of long touchdown runs, finishing the game with three carries for 105 yards and two scores. It earns him Rookie of the Week, marking the third time a Browns rookie has won the award, following Denzel Ward in Week 1 and Baker Mayfield in Week 3.

By the end of the season, that trio will win the award an unbelievable 11 times, with Mayfield winning seven times, and both Ward and Chubb doing so twice. The other 31 NFL teams combined would only win six times, with one coming on the Browns' bye week.

Week 5: Browns vs. Ravens

Baltimore enters this game with a franchise-record streak of 13 straight games with 20 or more points. Considering the Browns allowed 45 points in their last game, that streak should be pretty safe, right?

Nah.

Somehow, despite both teams going for over 400 total yards, only one touchdown is scored in the entire game, and Greg Joseph misses the extra point. The Browns make up for this by blocking a 48-yard attempt from Justin Tucker, the most accurate kicker in NFL history, before the half, meaning the Browns hold a 6–3 lead at the break.

After the Browns extended the lead to 9–3, Tucker got redemption with two second-half field goals, including a 32-yarder with 52 seconds left to tie it at nine. Joseph got a shot from 55 yards out to give the Browns the win in regulation, but you know how this goes by now — he misses. The Browns find themselves in overtime for the second consecutive week and a third time in five games.

Following a couple of punts, the Browns find themselves with 4th-and-5 at the Ravens' 39. A conversion would give them a great chance at the win, but to make things even more dramatic, the Browns turn the ball over. Luckily, they get it back in no time, and drive the field, giving Joseph another crack from 37 yards for the game as time expires. It's one of the ugliest game-winners you'll ever see, but the kick is good. Vindication. The Browns avoid a tie and take it, 12–9.

Believe it or not, this was the first time in a Browns game all season that the team ahead with three minutes left actually won the game. And even this one took overtime.

Congratulations, Cleveland! That's a multiple-win season for the first time in three years! The victory also marked the Browns' first win on a Sunday since Week 14 of 2015.

It was at this point that I really began to take notice of the insanity going on with this team. To recap, five weeks into the season, every Browns game had been decided by four points or less. Three had been to overtime. They had even tied!

Since the NFL instituted overtime in 1974, no team has tied twice in a season. The 2018 Cleveland Browns had already gone into the last two minutes of overtime three times.

All five games had been absolutely ludicrous. Missed kicks,

turnovers, lead changes — things had been completely unpredictable. During the week following the Ravens game, I wrote an article where I hypothesized that the football gods were confused.

After two decades of relentlessly torturing the Browns, maybe they felt they had gone too far? Now that the Browns had become a competent team, and fan favorites, should they continue to force Cleveland to suffer, or turn the Browns into champions?

Born from that uncertainty, the gods found a compromise — make every game chaotic. Five weeks into the season, the Browns were 2–2–1, but that record could have easily been either 5–0 or 0–5.

What would happen next?

Week 6: Browns vs. Chargers

Perhaps all the overtime had finally gotten to the Browns. Maybe the Chargers were simply a better team. Either way, the Browns were simply smashed in Week 6. The Chargers opened the scoring early and coasted to a 38–14 victory, the outcome never in doubt.

It would be Carlos Hyde's final game as a Brown. On the Friday following the loss, Hyde was shipped to Jacksonville in exchange for a 2019 5th round pick. The trade made Nick Chubb, who had been averaging an absurd 10.8 yards-per-attempt in limited action, the new starting running back. Despite only 16 carries in his first six games, Chubb would go on to finish the season with 1,145 scrimmage yards and 10 touchdowns.

Week 7: Browns @ Buccaneers

If Week 6 was a chance for fans to catch their breath, Week 7's encounter with the Bucs saw the Browns dial the insanity back up to 11. Let's do this one last time.

Despite opening up the scoring with a safety, the Browns trailed 16–2 at halftime. But as we've learned, no lead in a Browns game is safe. After each team put seven on the board in the third quarter, Cleveland scored two touchdowns in the fourth, tying the game at 23 shortly before the two-minute warning.

This gave Jameis Winston a chance to embark on a game-winning drive. Right on cue, he marched the Bucs offense to the Browns' 22, setting up Chandler Catanzaro with a 40-yard try to snap his team's three-game losing streak and atone for his missed extra point earlier in the game.

Wide right.

His attempt was from farther away than the 33-yard extra point but had the same result. As it would turn out, Catanzaro was still too close. His second miscue of the day sent the Browns to their fourth overtime in seven weeks.

Take that in. A fourth overtime. In case you were wondering, the record for most overtime games played in an entire season is five, set by the 1983 Packers. But now joining the group of teams in second place was the Browns, who needed only until October 21st to reach their fourth extra period.

And just like the first three, the Browns punt on their first possession. Luckily, Cleveland gets the ball back just yards outside of field goal range when Jamie Collins intercepts a Winston pass at the Bucs' 45. However, on the ensuing 3rd-and-3 from the 38, Baker Mayfield is sacked, losing the seven yards the Browns had gained on the previous play. Punt.

Similarly, the Bucs go three-and-out. It seems no one wants to win this game. Perhaps a bit of a push is required. At the end of a strong punt return, Jabrill Peppers fumbles the ball. Tampa Bay gets it back in Browns territory, on the 48-yard line.

Now, for one of the most heartbreaking sequences I can remember. On 3rd-and-3, Genard Avery is called for a neutral zone infraction, gifting the Bucs a first down at the 36. The Browns bear down. On first down, Myles Garrett sacks Winston for a huge loss of 12 yards. On second down, Larry Ogunjobi and Emmanuel Ogbah combine for another sack, bringing up 3rd-and-29 from the Bucs' own 45. Cleveland should get the ball back one last time.

Instead, Jameis Winston fires to DeSean Jackson for 14 yards, setting up Catanzaro with a 59-yard try, his second opportunity to end the game.

Money. It's the longest field goal ever kicked in overtime. When you're cursed like the Browns, not only do you lose — you do so in the most devastating ways possible. Bucs 26, Browns 23.

2–4–1. After everything — the opening tie, Mayfield heroics, and four overtimes, that's where the Browns stood. Last place in the AFC North, a game and a half behind all three other teams. If the first seven weeks of the 2018 season were a rollercoaster, the ride had broken in the middle of a loop, leaving the Cleveland Browns stranded upside down.

Out of the Dawg House

When a team loses, they make changes. After going winless the year before, the 2018 Browns arrived as a remarkably different team. However, despite all the alterations to the roster and coaching staff, one position was still curiously untouched — head coach.

Hue Jackson now stood 3–35–1 in his tenure with the Browns. Without a long leash to begin with, Jackson needed to turn things around immediately. His opportunity came in the form of a trip to Pittsburgh to face the Steelers, a team the Browns had tied less than two months prior.

This meeting would not be as close. A couple of first-quarter field goals gave the Browns an early 6–0 advantage, but outside of a fluke play where the Steelers forgot the rules and allowed the Browns to recover an onside kick off a safety punt, it was all Pittsburgh, who won 33–18.

That third straight loss would prove to be the nail in the coffin for Jackson, who was fired after the game along with his offensive coordinator Todd Haley. Unbelievably, Jackson became the sixth consecutive Browns head coach to be fired after his team's second game of the season against the Steelers.

Even when they aren't getting coaches canned, the Steelers have long aided the cause of Browns suffering. Who knocked the Browns out of the playoffs in their last postseason appearance after the 2002 season? The Steelers. What about their prior trip to the playoffs after the 1994 campaign? Also the Steelers. And of course, who beat the Browns in Week 17 of 2017 to set Cleveland's winless season in stone?

Once again, the Pittsburgh Steelers.

As fate would have it, In just over two months, the Steelers would need a Browns victory on the last day of the regular season to make the playoffs. But for now, the Browns were focused on salvaging their season with Gregg Williams, former defensive coordinator and newly promoted interim head coach, calling the shots.

In Williams' Week 9 debut, his Browns ran into the 7–1 Chiefs and the highest-scoring offense in the league, averaging over 36 points per game behind breakout star and eventual MVP of the league Patrick Mahomes. The game was the highly-anticipated rematch of a 2016 contest between Mahomes' Texas Tech Red Raiders and Baker Mayfield's Oklahoma Sooners which broke the NCAA record for combined offensive yards in a game.

Mayfield threw for 545 yards and seven touchdowns in that 66–59 Oklahoma victory, while Mahomes accounted for over 800 total yards by himself in a losing effort.

Mahomes would get revenge in their first NFL meeting. After the Browns kept things close through the first half, the Chiefs broke away in the third quarter and went on to win 37–21. It wasn't quite the legendary shootout of two years prior, but both quarterbacks had strong performances, looking like the future of the league.

That's all well and good, but the Browns were now 2–6–1 and in danger of wasting away in another lost season. Week 10, the team's final matchup before their bye week, was against the streaky Atlanta Falcons, who had won three straight coming in.

The Browns were six-point underdogs at home and staring at a potential fifth-consecutive loss. Yet, just as the league was ready to write them off, Cleveland put together their most impressive win of the season in a 28–16 triumph. It was an ultra-efficient day from Baker Mayfield, who finished 17/20 for 216 yards and three touchdowns.

Asked about it after the game, Mayfield delivered one of the most memorable quotes of the season, one that would come to define the team's mentality going forward.

"When I woke up this morning, I was feeling pretty dangerous."

Dangerous indeed. Led by a confident Mayfield and following their first November win in four years, the Browns would be able to rest and refuel on their bye week with hopes of making a late push.

But even on their bye week, the Browns didn't fail to entertain. On Sunday morning of Week 11, the NFL was stunned by a report from Adam Schefter that the Browns were interested in interviewing former Secretary of State Condoleezza Rice for their head coaching job.

No, seriously.

The rumor was eventually shot down, but both general manager John Dorsey and Rice herself had to issue statements on the matter. Say what you want, the Browns have a remarkable ability to stay in the headlines.

They were back in action in Week 12, with their first matchup of the season against the Bengals. Divisional rivalries are always a little more important, but this one was extra special. After being fired by the Browns, Hue Jackson had joined the Bengals as an assistant to head coach Marvin Lewis.

Unsurprisingly, the Browns didn't take kindly to that. Cleveland was already leading 21–0 in the second quarter when Damarious Randall intercepted Bengals quarterback Andy Dalton's pass.

Randall then handed the ball to his old coach on the Cincinnati sideline.

When time ran out, the Browns had won 35–20. It was a road victory, something Hue Jackson couldn't produce in two and a half seasons. It was also the franchise's first time winning back-to-back games in over four years.

With four more touchdowns from Baker Mayfield, Baker-mania really began to take over. By this point, even babies were being named after the promising young quarterback. Cleveland needed someone to believe in. Mayfield was that someone.

Turnovers led to a relatively uneventful loss in Houston the following week, but it wasn't enough to slow down the Browns' rhythm.

In Week 14, a late goal-line stand preserved a 26–20 win over the Panthers. The following Saturday, Cleveland won again, this time in Denver, snapping an 11-game losing streak against the Broncos dating back to 1990, before Art Modell relocated his team to Baltimore. Most of the modern Browns hadn't even been born then.

The game marked four wins in five weeks, equaling Cleveland's win total from 2015, 2016, and 2017 combined, giving Gregg Williams more wins as a Browns head coach in six games than Hue Jackson could manage in 40.

Speaking of Jackson, his Bengals came to FirstEnergy Stadium for a Week 16 rematch. With Jeff Driskel at quarterback for an injured Andy Dalton, the Browns entered as 8.5 point favorites, their most favorable spread since 2007.

Although Cleveland was officially eliminated from playoff contention the day before the game, their rematch with Cincy went almost exactly like the first meeting, with the Browns scoring the game's first 23 points before a late Bengals run brought the final score to 26–18,

It was a bad beat for gamblers, but a result that brought the Browns to .500, with a 7–7–1 record entering the final week of the season. Incredibly, the Browns had managed to turn it around.

Perhaps it had something to do with Hue Jackson's firing. After a strong start to the season, the Bengals had fallen apart in the second half of the year, their year an almost perfect inversion of the Browns'.

Without Jackson on their team, the Bengals and Browns had combined to win 10 games. With him, they won just three.

Week 17 would be symbolic. At 7–7–1, the Browns were going for their first winning season in 11 years. More than that, they had a chance to play spoiler. The AFC North race was down to two teams: the Baltimore Ravens and the Pittsburgh Steelers. Only one could make the playoffs. The Ravens held a half-game lead, but with the Steelers heavy favorites to beat the Bengals, the Browns had an opportunity to defeat the Ravens, the former Browns, and the team that left Cleveland, ending their season in the process.

It wouldn't make up for all the suffering caused by the relocation 22 years prior, but it would be a start. The Browns could finally escape their demons and emerge as a force to be reckoned with.

Judgment Day, Part II

The Steelers had done their part. And now, following their victory, the team stayed on Heinz Field, united with their fans, eyes glued to the video boards in the stadium. Chants of "LET'S GO BROWNS!" sounded loud, cheering on their divisional rivals playing in Baltimore, four hours away.

Cleveland had trailed by 13 points at halftime, but now, with less than two minutes to play, that deficit was just two. Ravens 26, Browns 24. The ball was in Baker Mayfield's hands, with his team needing only a field goal to win their fourth-straight game, sending them above .500 and their opponents out of play-off position.

The drive started at the Browns' own 26. After an incomplete pass to Breshad Perriman, Mayfield went to Perriman again on second down for a 19-yard pickup, which stood after a lengthy review.

The next two plays went almost the same way. An incompletion to Jarvis Landry, and then a 16-yard gain to Landry. This one was initially ruled incomplete as well but was reversed after another tension-building review. When the dust settled, the Browns had 1st-and-10 from the Ravens' 39.

Incomplete pass. Incomplete pass. Incomplete pass.

Three straight missed connections brought 4th-and-10. Cleveland had two options: send out Greg Joseph for a 57-yard try or go for it. Joseph had missed a 46-yard attempt at the end of the first half, and due to either lack of confidence, lack of leg, or trust in Mayfield, the Browns offense stayed on the field.

Unsurprisingly, the Ravens brought a blitz. As six men in purple and black rushed Mayfield, the Browns QB was forced to get rid of the ball quickly. He threw in the direction of Duke Johnson, who was on a slant route, but Pro Bowl linebacker C.J. Mosley made a great read on the play, tipping and intercepting the ball before it could reach its destination. From that point on, all the Ravens had to do was kneel.

The #1 defense in football had gotten their stop and earned themselves a division title and a spot in the postseason. For the Cleveland Browns, redemption would have to wait once again.

A New Cleveland Browns

Perhaps disappointment would be an apt initial reaction to the loss in Baltimore, but after taking a step back and evaluating the Cleveland Browns' 2018 season as a whole, it would be impossible to label it anything other than a resounding success.

Just one year after being the absolute laughingstock of the league, a team that failed to win a single game, the Browns went 7–8–1. It was their best overall record since 2007 and the first time they finished outside of last place in the AFC North since 2010.

However, that third-place division finish doesn't tell the whole story of just how close to really making waves the Browns actually were. If they had only beaten the Steelers instead of tying in Week 1 and closed out that final drive against the Ravens in Week 17, the Browns, Steelers, and Ravens would have all finished at 9–7. With a 5–1 division record, Cleveland would have won the tiebreaker, made the playoffs, and hosted a game on Wild Card Weekend. They were that close.

Throughout the season, the team's rookie core had shined. Baker Mayfield set a new rookie record with 27 passing touchdowns, even after missing the first two and a half games of the year. Corner Denzel Ward was a Pro Bowler in his debut season, and Nick Chubb accounted for well over 1100 scrimmage yards and 10 touchdowns despite backing up Carlos Hyde until Week 7.

Second-year pass rusher Myles Garrett finished with 13.5 sacks, turning into one of the league's most feared men. He, along with guard Joel Bitonio and wide receiver Jarvis Landry, joined Ward in the Pro Bowl.

In 2017, the Browns finished with a -28 turnover differential, the worst such mark in the Super Bowl era. In 2018, the Browns were +7, and second in the league with 31 takeaways.

By the second half of the season, this team was rolling, and the momentum didn't stop there.

After promoting new head coach Freddie Kitchens and signing a highly-desired coordinator tandem of Todd Monken and Steve Wilks, the Browns made perhaps the biggest move of the 2019 offseason by trading for Giants star wideout Odell Beckham Jr.

This paired Beckham with his college teammate and best friend in Jarvis Landry to catch balls from a rising star in Baker Mayfield. And for just Jabrill Peppers, a 1st rounder, and a 3rd rounder, most saw the trade as a steal for the Browns.

Cleveland also signed running back Kareem Hunt, although he would be suspended the first eight games of 2019 for violating the league's personal conduct policy from a domestic violence incident. The Browns kept adding on talent, while the divisional rival Steelers lost both of their stars, Le'Veon Bell and Antonio Brown.

As the offseason continued, the hype around the Browns only kept building. All of a sudden, they were not only divisional favorites, but among the list of projected Super Bowl contenders. Entering training camp, the Browns had jumped all the way to 12–1 title odds, tied for fifth-best in the entire NFL and trailing only the four teams that reached the Conference Championships in 2018.

Perhaps this was taking things too quickly for a team that had still never won a playoff game in franchise history post-relocation or even produced a single .500 season in the last decade.

Then again, maybe not. If they could turn around the entire attitude surrounding a team which had lost for nearly two decades straight in one season, who's to say they can't win the Super Bowl in the next?

There's something undeniably amazing going on in Cleveland right now, and it has the whole football world watching. The Browns have fielded great teams before, and they Mayfield a great team again soon.

Author's Note: Maybe next year? In 2019, what started as a season with just about the highest expectations a Browns season could have quickly fell flat. The Browns struggled with penalties, turnovers, and poor play calling while Baker Mayfield took a step backward in his second year.

Perhaps the most notable event from Cleveland's season, and the one that best encapsulates the team's lack of discipline, came during their Week 11 matchup with the Steelers. In the closing seconds of the game, Myles Garrett got into a brawl with Pittsburgh quarterback Mason Rudolph which ended with Garrett removing Rudolph's helmet and striking him with it. As a result, Garrett was handed an indefinite suspension.

In Week 17, the Browns would fall to the 1-14 Bengals, ultimately finishing with a 6-10 record while the Ravens finished 14-2, earning the #1 seed in the AFC. After the season, both coach Freddie Kitchens and general manager John Dorsey were fired.

What can I say? Browns will be Browns.

IV: ON RULES AND STRUCTURE

A RADICAL PROPOSAL TO MODIFY THE NBA THREE-POINTER

Originally published: Jan 31, 2019

It's no secret that the NBA is undergoing a three-point revolution. Fueled by the analytics movement and sharpshooters like Stephen Curry, teams this season are shooting an average of 31.3 threes per game, an over 50% increase from just six seasons ago when teams fired 20 shots from behind the arc per contest.

In the modern NBA, more than one in three shots taken is a three-pointer. Last season, the Houston Rockets became the first team to ever take more threes than twos in a season, an astounding statistic for a shot that once seemed more like a gimmick than anything else. Just a couple weeks ago, the Rockets fired a record 70 threes in a single game against the Nets.

While expanded use of the three-point shot has led to a faster-paced, higher-scoring, and arguably more interesting game to the common fan, many traditionalists would argue the heavy emphasis on flashy three-point shooting is eroding fundamental basketball, and that the league should move back the three-point line to combat the distance shooting evolution.

Personally, I don't subscribe to this idea that we need to move the line back; three-point shooting percentages league-wide have remained essentially the same over the past 20 years. However, I have recently heard a very intriguing proposal to add a new element of strategy to the three-ball.

That idea? Allow home teams to decide where to place the three-point line. You heard me right. Under this idea, a team could decide to paint the line 28 feet away from the basket or play with FIBA rules and set it at 22 feet 1 3/4 inches. There could potentially be 30 different arcs.

As a hypothetical, this idea is so much fun. It could completely change the game, and at a bare minimum, it's a unique and highly creative concept. But before you rule it out as a serious change, there is some precedent for different playing field dimensions in major sports.

Just take a look at baseball, where each stadium has different home run distances. The MLB's only rules are that newly built stadiums must have left and right-field foul poles at least 325 feet away from home plate and that center field measures at least 400 feet. In the MLS, pitches can measure from 110–120 yards long and 70–80 yards wide, leaving the largest fields with more than 16% more surface area than Yankee Stadium, home to New York City FC.

Although each court has the same dimensions, even the current NBA three-point line isn't uniform, with a 23-foot 9–inch arc that goes down to 22 feet in the corners.

In this system, the NBA would likely set a minimum and maximum three-point distance and require teams to submit their chosen dimensions before the season. This is where we could see some interesting strategic decisions.

If you're a poor shooting team, would you move the line back to try to take the three-point shot out of the game for your opponents, or bring it in closer to help your team make more threes?

What if you're a good shooting team?

This might seem paradoxical, but I think if you're an above-average three-point shooting, you should actually move the line closer, while poor shooting teams should move it further back.

Let's think about this from the perspective of the Golden State Warriors, leaders of the three-point explosion. Sure, guys like Stephen Curry and Klay Thompson are capable of hitting 30-footers, but these are not the most efficient shots possible. Moving the line back to that distance would essentially eliminate the three-pointer from your opponents' arsenal, but it would also restrict your three-point offense to maybe a couple of Curry bombs per game.

If you have the best distance shooters in the league, you want to maximize your advantage by increasing the number of threes taken per game, which would mean moving the line closer to the basket. I think a distance of 20-22 feet would be optimal, as you wouldn't want to move it so close that current mid-range shots become threes.

For poorer shooting teams, I would suggest moving the line back to at least 25 feet. That's the distance where we start to see a noticeable drop in shooting percentages compared to shots from any other distance outside of three feet. More importantly, though, and this is really the benefit of a 25-foot three-point line, it eliminates the corner three, as a basketball court is only 50 feet wide.

Without the corner three, the three-point shot becomes way easier to defend – it's now a less efficient shot solely from the backcourt. There's less space to defend and less space for the offense to operate in to generate these shots. And because defenses wouldn't be as worried about guarding the corners, we could see the zone defense come back into style.

Since we know the mid-range is the least efficient place to score, in an NBA with fewer threes, the emphasis would return to play out of the post and inside the paint, which should favor teams that don't specialize in the three. At the very least, if every shot becomes worth two points, we'll see decreases in scoring and tempo, increasing variance and helping bottom dwellers.

Of course, this all assumes the NBA sets specific rules for how short or long the three-point shot can be. But strict specification is boring, so let's just go nuts with this idea.

Want to eliminate threes entirely? Make the three-point line 40 feet! Giannis and Ben Simmons become the most valuable players in the league! What if you could make the restricted area or just dunks worth three, and everything else worth two? Now that's how you bring back the era of dominant centers! You could allow hotspots or unevenly drawn lines. Allow teams to tailor their line game-to-game to match their opponent. What if the three-point line was only in play for the fourth quarter or moved closer in the fourth to increase comeback potential? I don't see any reason why the NBA would adopt these rules, but they would definitely spice things up and open the door for more court-specific rules.

Lastly, some secondary effects of allowing teams to choose their own three-point distance. It would make analytical comparisons more difficult, as the lack of three-point equivalency would inflate the stats of those playing in courts with shorter lines, similar to how shorter fences lead to inflated home run totals in the MLB.

The changes would also lead to stronger home-court advantages, unique draft and free agency strategies, and overall a bit more parity in the league, which I think are probably (?) good things.

I wouldn't expect to see the NBA hurry to make any changes to the three-point line, seeing as the league is at an all-time high in popularity, but it's certainly an enjoyable idea and one that could add another level of strategy into an increasingly complex league.

Editor's Note: Over the past year, I have changed my stance on modifying the three-point line. While shooting percentages from behind the arc may be consistent over time, the fact that analytics has proven threes to be more efficient than most two-point shots has led to an increase in three-point attempts and players shooting threes, resulting in a loss in diversity of offensive styles.

Many fans may still enjoy seeing a high-volume of three-point shots, but when the future is clearly trending towards a league where half of shots taken (or even more) are threes, something should be done to help maintain balance and give life back to the mid-range and post play.

Is letting teams choose their own three-point line the solution? Probably not, although I still love talking about the idea. We shouldn't be afraid to discuss radical solutions to problems. Moving the three-point line back to 25 feet would be a good start, although there are many possible options...

FIFA MADE THE RIGHT DECISION TO KEEP THE 2022 WORLD CUP AT 32 TEAMS...BUT FOR THE WRONG REASONS

Originally published: May 22, 2019

FIFA announced Wednesday that it has decided not to expand the 2022 World Cup in Qatar from 32 to 48 teams. Soccer's international governing body cited concerns about the ability to prepare another nation to co-host the event in time, a necessity with the change, and the possible logistical and human rights impacts on the region as reasons against a 48-team tournament.

Certainly, FIFA has made the correct decision here. There simply wasn't enough time to create a feasible plan to pull off an expanded World Cup, a push that was only publicly made this year. But it wasn't for a lack of trying – FIFA President Gianni Infantino even held talks in Kuwait last month in an attempt to get the country to host matches in 2022. If Infantino could have made things work, he would have. And therein lies the problem.

Applaud FIFA for their decision to keep the 2022 World Cup at 32 teams all you want. It only prolongs the inevitable move to a 48-team tournament already slated for 2026, despite the fact that a World Cup with 48 teams is a terrible idea.

Infantino first announced his ambition back in late 2016 to expand the World Cup to 48 teams starting in 2026. The proposal was then unanimously agreed upon by the FIFA council in January 2017. Back then, I was strongly against the idea. The reasons why have not changed in the time since.

Disguised as a plan to satisfy fans globally by allowing more countries to be represented during soccer's biggest event, World Cup expansion is a play by FIFA for money and power. FIFA can expect to generate an extra $1 billion in revenue from the 2026 World Cup alone while adding teams will satisfy individual regions by giving them more World Cup spots and more cash.

Even worse, it comes at a cost to the quality of the tournament itself. The 48-team World Cup results in 16 groups of three teams, of which the top two teams in each advance to create a 32-team field for the tournament's knockout phase. This new group format is where the issues arise.

First off, the addition of 16 teams will dilute the overall quality of play in the group stage, leading to situations where one team will be clearly weaker than the other two and subjected to blowouts.

One might ask, "but isn't there hardly any difference between the 32nd and 33rd-best teams in the world?" Unfortunately, that isn't how it plays out.

Each region (or continent, effectively) is given a specific number of spots in the tournament. This allows each region to be represented but does not ensure all the best 32 nations compete in the World Cup. Even if all 32 of the world's best came from UEFA (Europe; and a good number of them do), only a fraction of those teams would make the field.

In 2018, Japan made the World Cup despite a world ranking of 61. Adding 16 teams would only further this issue, leaving many groups to have predictable results. Some matches might even be practically pointless, as I explained back in 2016.

"A three-team group requires three matches to be played: A vs. B, A vs. C, and B vs. C. Let's say, for example, that in the first two group games, team A loses to both B and C. In this scenario, by the time B and C play each other, they are both guaranteed to advance. This could lead to the teams resting their best players, placing a higher emphasis on staying healthy and fit for their Round of 32 matches than winning the current game."

This three-match group stage also invites a problem of some teams having a rest advantage over others. In the current World Cup format, each group plays a round-robin against three other teams for a total of six games. These games are played in pairs, happening on either the same day or within one day of each other. The final two matches of each group are played on the same day.

Having only three games means one team is resting while the other two teams play. Consider the above situation, where a three-team group plays the following games: A vs. B, A vs. C, and B vs. C. In the second match, C has an advantage over A because A has played recently while C got to rest and scout A. In the third match, B has this same advantage over C.

Overall, B benefits from having a rest gap in between their two games, a luxury not given to the other teams. C is aided once and harmed once, and A is only harmed by having to play back-to-back in the group's first two matches.

Even worse, team A might suffer from match-fixing as a result of their group schedule. Again, here's how I put it back in 2016.

"What would happen if... team A drew 1-1 against both B and C? Team A would be left with two points, while B and C would each have just one entering the match with each other. Should one team win the game, the other would be eliminated from the tournament. To ensure both squads advance, they could agree to draw 2-2, leaving all three teams with two points, but giving B and C the edge in terms of goals scored for the tiebreaker."

Infantino has suggested replacing ties with penalty kicks to help deal with this issue, but it wouldn't fully solve the problem, as teams could still finish with one win and loss each and with identical numbers of goals scored and conceded. Plus, is an idea really worth taking on if it means eliminating ties completely, replacing them with arbitrary shootouts?

Reducing the group stage from three games to two would also increase variance, meaning that one bad performance could leave teams all but eliminated. This concern doesn't quite rise to the level of match-fixing, but it's worth noting that just two games is arguably an inadequate amount of time to determine the best teams in a group.

The existing 32-team World Cup format has proven itself to be perfect since its inception in 1998. While more nations may be able to experience the joy of participating in the World Cup by expanding the field to 48 teams, doing so would wreck the structure of the tournament, leaving the group stage susceptible to lopsided matches, unfair rest advantages, and potential match-fixing. The quality of play would decrease, and variance would increase.

If holding the best tournament is your objective rather than making the most money, World Cup expansion isn't the way to go.

SHOULD WE GET RID OF FIVE-SET TENNIS MATCHES?

Originally published: May 25, 2019

When the French Open begins next week, it will feature one of the more curious rules in sports, one that has become so normalized that we hardly recognize it at all. While men's matches will be played as best-of-five sets, women's matches will only be a best-of-three.

The reason why largely stems from longstanding beliefs that women were not as physically capable as men. Across all sports, this view was dominant until at least the last half-century, with the effects still felt today. In a tennis context, it suggests women would be unable to play five sets at a high quality. If there is even any truth to that, there certainly isn't to the extent that people believed when the three-set match for women was standardized.

A few people here and there have raised concerns about the discrepancy, pointing out the sexism behind the rule and asking for both genders to play matches of the same length, but there has been no major movement for change. However, a very interesting argument can be made due to tennis' progressive equal pay structure.

In 2007, Wimbledon became the last Grand Slam to award equal prize money to the men's and women's tournaments, and tennis has been rightly applauded for achieving gender equality – at least in this area. There are still imbalances in tennis leadership,

106

as well as greater promotion and time featured on main courts favoring men, but compared to other sports, tennis is a leader in overall equality.

But if both genders are paid equally on the basis of equal pay for equal work, it raises the question: is the work actually equal when men play more sets? Novak Djokovic has suggested that men might deserve to make more for a different reason, citing the increased popularity and revenue generated by the men's game.

The viability of these arguments depends on our definition of equal work. If we only look at the number of sets that are played, then men do more work. But some sports have built-in gender differences. Women's tees in golf are slightly shorter than the men's, but they still play eighteen holes. If we view tennis in the same vein, women and men still have to win seven matches to become a Grand Slam champion. This would suggest there is indeed equal work.

Djokovic's argument is the most complicated one. Sport popularity and revenue generation is a popular counter to the U.S. Women's National Soccer Team's fight for equal pay. These people claim that despite the women's incredible success (particularly in comparison to the U.S. Men's National Team), since the women's game doesn't bring in the same revenue, they shouldn't make as much.

But how can women ever be expected to generate the same attention as men if they aren't given the same resources?

I'm not sure what the answer here is. If male professional tennis players banded together and demanded higher pay than women, it would be highly controversial and send shockwaves through the sport. All I know is that I wouldn't want to be the one to make a ruling.

Historically, there is a precedent for both women playing five sets and men playing three. Women's matches were five sets in WTA championships from 1984 to 1998, and in the U.S. Open from 1894 to 1901. Men play just three sets in nearly every setting outside of the four Grand Slams but even played three sets in early rounds of Grand Slams back in the 1970s.

Women going up to five sets would likely only lead to scheduling nightmares, as match lengths are far more unpredictable with five sets, and scheduling Grand Slams is already difficult enough for the men's game as is. A far more reasonable solution would be to eliminate five-set matches entirely, creating a uniform three-set format for professional tennis matches everywhere.

Aside from easier scheduling and equivalence with the women's game, three-set matches would potentially be safer for men. Five-set matches can take a toll on the body, and those extra sets add up over the course of a two-week tournament. The heat can also be an issue and has forced many players to retire in recent years.

Fifth-set tiebreakers can also be problematic. Rather than play a traditional tiebreak when the game score reaches 6-6 in a set, Grand Slams have traditionally played on until one player wins by two games.

This has led to some ridiculously long matches, especially featuring American John Isner, who is known for his strong serve, leading to matches with few break games.

In 2010, Isner played Nicolas Mahut in the first round of Wimbledon. The fifth set took three days to complete, with Isner eventually winning 70-68. 70-68! In total, the match lasted over 11 hours. In the semifinals of Wimbledon in 2018, Isner fell to Kevin Anderson 26-24 in the fifth set of a 6-hour, 36-minute match.

Clearly, matches this long feature a high risk to players, and should not be allowed. In the aftermath of the Isner-Anderson match, Wimbledon and the Australian Open changed their fifth-set tiebreak rules. The Australian Open adopted the traditional tiebreak, while Wimbledon goes to a tiebreak at 12-12. The French Open, however, still has no fifth-set tiebreak.

Despite the safety argument, a switch to three-set Grand Slams will likely not occur any time soon. The spectacle of five sets leads to greater tension and fan appeal. Especially on TV, where matches can take up more time and draw higher ratings, a reduction to three sets is unappealing.

Five sets also allow for more time to determine the best player. This generation has seen the total dominance of Djokovic, Rafael Nadal, and Roger Federer, largely for this reason. In the women's game, there is higher variance making it more difficult to win Grand Slams.

Of course, the number one reason holding back a change is simply tradition. People generally like things the way they are, and players don't want to look weak or out of shape by advocating for playing three sets.

But the argument is certainly there. Three-set tennis matches at Grand Slams may reduce injuries and lead to fairness between men and women. For now, though, we can still root for an exciting, best-of-5 final in the men's singles.

FOUR OVERPOWERED RULES IN SPORTS AND HOW WE CAN FIX THEM

Originally published: July 14, 2019

Every time I watch a soccer match, I quietly hope neither team is awarded a penalty kick. Penalty shootouts to decide a game still tied after regulation and extra time are fine, but penalties during play have never sat well with me.

Knowing that an average game only has around three goals (one or two per team), awarding a penalty kick — a direct shot on goal from 12 yards away with a roughly 75% conversion rate — seems wildly unbalanced.

In a scoreless match, a single penalty can lead a team to victory. Other times, it can provide a decisive winner or allow a team to tie things up without scoring in normal play. Giving the opposing team a penalty is an exceedingly strong punishment for a foul in the box, considering how few goals are actually scored.

It also encourages players to "flop" or "dive", intentionally falling down in the penalty area with the intention of drawing a penalty. Players know that even if they don't get the call most of the time, they're still better off fishing for that penalty kick. The goal of soccer — and all sports — should be to score, not to trick the officials.

Yet, some rules do just that — incentivizing teams to try to draw fouls or even play for the tie rather than the win. Let's propose rule changes to fix these problems.

Penalty Kicks

As I've already stated, penalty kicks are too valuable and have only worsened the flopping epidemic. You can't eliminate them completely — that would only lead to increased mugging inside the box, and potentially even handballs to stop goals a la Luis Suárez in the 2010 World Cup.

I see two options here. The first would be to make penalties worth only half a goal. That way, it could be a decider if both teams scored the same amount of goals in regular play, but otherwise, the team with more actual goals would win.

For example, if a game was 0–0, a team could win .5–0 with a penalty. But if both teams had scored twice, the team who had one goal by penalty would fall 2–1.5.

The other option is to make the penalty kick taken from a further distance, therefore lowering the odds of scoring on one. Currently, kicks are taken from 12 yards away. But what if they were 15 or 18 yards away? Either would help devalue the penalty.

Red Cards

Another rule in soccer I disagree with is the red card rule. If a player receives a red card (or two yellow cards), they are sent off the pitch, essentially ejected from the match. But instead of their team getting to send in a replacement, they have to spend the whole rest of the match with one fewer player than their opponents. It's 11 on 10.

Talk about excessive. Rarely do teams a player down score in the remainder of the match. If they were ahead or tied prior to the red card, they usually just go on the defensive, trying to preserve that win or draw. Teams absolutely deserve to be penalized for committing fouls, but a man down for the rest of the game seems ridiculous.

I like how hockey does it. When someone commits a penalty, the other team goes on a power play. Soccer could have a similar system. Regular fouls could result in one or two-minute power plays. Yellow cards five. Red cards fifteen. That player would be ineligible to return, but the team could substitute someone in their place.

This change would make players more reluctant to commit fouls while preserving the overall fairness of the game.

Three-Point Shooting Fouls

James Harden knows a secret. The most efficient play in the NBA isn't a dunk, as most people think it is. It's a three-point shooting foul. While a breakaway Giannis slam is worth two points, if Harden can get fouled on a three, he can earn 2.6 points on average. Even average free throw shooters will earn more than two points if given three tries.

Just like penalty kicks and red cards, players are incentivized to play to draw whistles. Over the last three NBA seasons, Harden has drawn 288 fouls on threes. The Hornets, the team with the second-most three-point fouls drawn, has 185.

I concede that this is a more difficult rule to change. If fouls on twos warrant two free throws, it logically follows that fouls on threes — which are also much rarer — should be worth three points. But for someone like Harden, who can draw whistles from behind the arc at ludicrous rates compared to everyone else, it's game-breaking. No play should be worth more than a dunk.

So, once again, there are two options. You could make three-point shooting fouls worth two points, but then it's not much better than just shooting the three. With the penalty reduced, it could lead to more fouls on threes, especially against poor free throw shooters like Lonzo Ball. Hack-a-Shaq is painful enough. No one wants to see Hack-a-Lonzo on the long ball.

Instead, a happy medium would be to penalize three-point fouls by giving the shooter one free throw and letting that team keep the ball. Treat it like a technical foul, minus the actual technical.

With this rule, teams would never want to foul a three-point shooter. It's still more severe than fouling a two-point shooter, but it will decrease flopping by shooters and end the 2.6 points per possession loophole.

Hockey's Overtime Loss

The NHL's scoring system is broken — plain and simple. This has nothing to do with officiating — it's far worse. The fact of the matter is that the optimal strategy for the NHL regular season is to play for the tie.

In the past, the NHL awarded two points for a win, one point for a tie, and no points for a loss. However, they decided that ties are boring and that instead, we needed to decide games in overtime.

That's fine. What is not fine is how they changed the scoring to accommodate such a change. Teams still get two points for wins and zero for losses, but now, each team is given one point for making it to overtime, and the team that wins in OT is given a second point.

Ties are gone. Overtime wins count the same as normal wins, and losses in that extra period are called, well, overtime losses (OTL). What makes this so ridiculous is that while games decided in regulation are worth two points, games that reach overtime are worth three, two to the winner and one to the loser.

In soccer, ties are discouraged, as they only award each team one point (two total), while a winner three. The NHL's rule does the opposite. If you can take every game to overtime, you can guarantee one point in each game and then play for the win.

Let's look at this in practice. The NHL season has 82 games. If you took each game into overtime and then won half, you would finish with 123 total points. In 2018–19, that would've been easily good enough for second-best in the league, even though you technically lost half your games.

But let's take it a step further. Say you were a really bad team who cut deals with all the other teams in the league to guarantee a point and then decide things in overtime. Then, you won just 20 of 82 games in OT, for a total of 102 points. That would still put you in sixth place out of the 30 teams in the league.

There is an unbelievably obvious way to solve this problem. Award three points for regulation wins, two for overtime wins, one for overtime losses, and zero for regulation losses. Overtime doesn't have to change, but now every game is worth a total of three points, and teams that win in regulation are rewarded for doing so.

In many ways, I am a sports traditionalist who likes things the way they are. However, some rules, even unintentionally, go against the integrity of the game. When that happens, changes need to be made.

DO MAJOR NORTH AMERICAN SPORTS LEAGUES HAVE TOO MANY TEAMS?

Originally published: July 20, 2019

It seems that for the major North American sports leagues, expansion is always on the mind. Perhaps this is indicative of a uniquely American mindset — a remnant of Manifest Destiny that requires every city to have its own professional sports teams.

Regardless, the NFL, NBA, MLB, NHL, and MLS have never been shy about growing bigger and bigger, with a steady adding of franchises over time in each league.

The most recent of these new teams is FC Cincinnati, which became the MLS' 24th team this year. As the youngest of the major leagues, Major League Soccer has been rapidly introducing new expansion teams with no signs of slowing down. In 2020, clubs in Miami and Nashville will begin play. Austin FC starts in 2021 as the MLS' 27th franchise, and the league has already announced its intention to jump to 30 teams in the coming years.

Elsewhere, the NHL brought hockey to the desert in 2017 with the Las Vegas Golden Knights and will set up shop in Seattle for the 2021–22 season, completing their expansion to 32 teams. The MLB is similarly looking to grow from 30 to 32 franchises, and commissioner Rob Manfred has even named potential destinations.

Expansion isn't even limited to the United States and Canada. Since 2007, the NFL has hosted at least one game internationally each year, with four in London and one in Mexico City scheduled for 2019. There isn't a poorer held secret in sports than the NFL's intentions to put a team in the United Kingdom.

The least likely of the five leagues to add more teams is the NBA. Yet, even NBA commissioner Adam Silver acknowledges that expansion of his league is inevitable. While it's not a major focus right now, it's only a matter of time before a team returns to Seattle, and once a 31st team comes to fruition, a 32nd won't be far behind.

For these leagues, bigger certainly seems to be better — but should that be the case? I want to suggest the idea that these leagues are actually too big, and that getting rid of teams would improve the overall product.

I'm usually against expansion, but until recently, I had never considered downsizing, mostly because it never seemed like a real option. And, to be clear, it isn't. Having more teams means more games and more money. Unless a league starts to struggle financially, teams aren't going to disband. Heavy expansion fees mean owners would want more teams, and for players, it leads to more available jobs.

Despite the infeasibility, let's consider the outcomes of eliminating teams. First, it would directly lead to greater competition. The teams that would be removed wouldn't be the LAs, New Yorks, or Bostons of the world. It would be the Jacksonvilles, Memphises, and Tampa Bays.

Especially in a sport without a salary cap like baseball, smaller market teams who can't afford the same payrolls as the Yankees or Dodgers are at a huge disadvantage. Every now and again, someone can break through — we all know the story of *Moneyball* — but over time, the same teams win again and again.

Even in salary cap sports, bigger markets are more likely to sign big-name free agents. Getting rid of small of the smaller teams would lead to more excitement. There would be more stars on each team, and attendance would be higher. Plus, your favorite team would win more.

Live sports attendance is dropping pretty much across the board and adding teams in medium to small markets won't help. 30 and 32 aren't magic numbers calculated to represent a perfect league size. Those are just the numbers we seem to have settled on over the past few decades.

Just because you can stick an MLB team in Portland doesn't mean you should. We don't need more franchises like Miami who struggle to average even 10,000 fans in a stadium that seats more than 36,000.

Some recent expansions have made sense — the Houston Texans, for example, have been a great success. But that was an obvious move. There are seven million people in the Houston metro area, and it's in Texas. Hockey in the desert with the Las Vegas Golden Knights has also worked, although it remains to be seen how the fanbase will hold up when the team isn't as competitive.

Others, however...not so much. Plenty of cities have teams but don't need them. This is especially true in MLS, which is already larger than just about every major league in the world. Most leagues have 16–20 teams. 30, like MLS is shooting for, is unheard of. And honestly, we just don't have the talent to support that many teams.

The MLS is being held back from growing to its full potential and rivaling other leagues around the world by its unending desire to add new clubs. This expansion would make sense if a promotion-relegation system was adopted, and the MLS could find a way to merge with the United Soccer League (USL). However, from both a business perspective and its clashes with the American mentality, that's unlikely to ever occur.

For my final takes, I would say that the MLB and MLS are too big, and all the other leagues are probably okay where they are if they don't expand. However, that's a big "if". When it comes to doing what's best and making money, money usually wins.

Author's Note: MLS has now finalized its expansion to 30 teams, with a team in Charlotte starting in 2021 alongside Austin F.C., and Sacramento and St. Louis franchises debuting in 2022. Can we stop now?

THE LITTLE LEAGUE WORLD SERIES DOESN'T NEED TO EXPAND

Originally published: August 30, 2019

On August 24, Little League Baseball announced that the Little League World Series (LLWS) will be expanding from 16 to 20 teams beginning in 2021.

Now, as someone who has written that the World Cup shouldn't grow to 48 teams, argued that North American sports leagues might be too big, and even published an entire short story warning against March Madness expansion, I predictably don't think that a 20-team LLWS is the greatest idea.

But before I make my case, let's go through the changes coming to everyone's favorite youth sports tournament.

These four new spots come in the form of two new United States regions and two international spots, meaning 10 U.S. and 10 international teams will now compete for the championship in Williamsport.

On the U.S. side, the Mountain region will include Montana, Nevada, Utah, and Wyoming, while the Metro region will feature teams from Connecticut, New Jersey, New York, and Rhode Island.

Both new international slots will feature teams from the Caribbean. While currently just one spot in the tournament is allocated to the Caribbean, starting in 2021, two automatic spots will rotate between Cuba, Panama, and Puerto Rico, with the third team still getting a chance to qualify through the existing Caribbean tournament.

At first thought, the expansion to 20 teams might seem like a good idea, and a way to allow more kids to enjoy the amazing atmosphere that is the LLWS. This is the classic argument for expansion — the increase in opportunity to join in on the fun. Whether it's for the FIFA World Cup, March Madness, or even just giving a city a new team, growth allows more people to take part.

It's a legitimate point, and if things ended there, I wouldn't have any problems with growing the LLWS. However, we would be foolish to think that the LLWS will stop at 20 teams. If they can pull that off, they'll move to 24, and 28, and 32.

When you're expanding, things get politicized quickly. Who will get the new regions? More teams mean more games — games that will be televised and bring in revenue. Injecting money into anything leads to a natural diminishing of moral values. I don't want to see the LLWS become more focused on profit than the kids.

Little League has committed $15 million to renovate its campuses, which should enhance the experience and ensure a smooth transition. Still, I worry about the consequences of growing the tournament, especially with the already notable cheating scandals, such as with Danny Almonte or the Jackie Robinson West Little League.

If things are going to expand, I question the choices for the new regions. We should want the most diverse field possible. However, by creating even narrower American regions and feeding both new international spots to the Caribbean, we fail to do that.

Some of the new regions look incredibly weak. We now have a Northwest region consisting of Alaska, Idaho, Oregon, and Washington and a Mountain region of Montana, Nevada, Utah, and Wyoming. Somehow, these are two distinct regions, while all of Europe and Africa have to share one spot. Can't we at least get a team from each continent?

From a strict gameplay perspective, having 20 teams doesn't make any sense, either. The LLWS employs a double-elimination format with winners and losers brackets on both the U.S. and international sides of the bracket.

The current format works because the total number of teams — 16 — is a power of two. After the first game, winners can play winners, and losers can play losers. 2–0 teams can play each other, as can 1–1 teams. Everything makes sense.

With 10 teams on each side of the field, after the initial games, an 0–1 team will be forced to face a 1–0 team. Then, should the 1–0 team win, there will only be seven teams in that pool from the original 10, which leads to all kinds of matchmaking issues.

It remains to be seen what the solution to this will be. All we know is that Little League says the tournament will retain its modified double-elimination format while adding an extra day onto the schedule to accommodate the increased number of teams.

A 20-team Little League World Series causes structural difficulties for the tournament and only paves the way for increased expansion which goes against the values of Little League baseball.

We don't need a larger tournament, and we don't need to expose our children to such a high-stress, televised environment focused on wins and losses. That's for the love of money, not the game.

THE MLB SHOULD NOT ADAPT THE MERCY RULE

Originally published: August 31, 2019

Earlier this month, one day after a brutal 19–5 defeat at the hands of the Cleveland Indians, New York Yankees manager Aaron Boone had some interesting words to say about a potential rule change for Major League Baseball — one which would've ended his team's blowout loss early.

Asked about the MLB possibly implementing a mercy rule, Boone said the idea was "worth exploring," and could be used to prevent late-game situations where position players pitch to preserve pitchers' arms and prevent injuries.

That relatively common scenario is tantamount to throwing in the towel, and no matter how exciting it can be for fans and the Cut4 Twitter account to see position players pitch, with the game virtually decided, a mercy rule could be used to end the suffering early and let everyone go home.

No point in wasting effort on a lost cause, right?

The mercy rule is notably used currently in Little League baseball and the Little League World Series (LLWS), where the normal six-inning game is ended if one team holds a 15-run lead after three innings, or a 10-run advantage after at least four innings. The likely implementation in MLB would be to end games featuring 10-run leads starting after the seventh inning.

However, it would be ridiculous for the MLB to start using the mercy rule as a way to end games, as it was never intended for use in a professional league setting.

The mercy rule only makes sense in situations where one team is so overmatched that playing a full game wouldn't make any sense. It works in Little League because teams routinely get matched up against far inferior opponents and smoke them, like when Japan put 20 runs on the board against Italy in this year's LLWS.

It even works in the World Baseball Classic (WBC), because although the hope is that the event will be more competitive, the possibility for severe mismatches still exists, such as in 2006, when the United States beat South Africa 17–0 in a game that luckily only lasted five innings.

Additionally, in an international tournament like the WBC, it's worth mentioning that you don't want players to be injured, leaving them unable to play for their regular teams.

However, these concerns don't apply to the MLB, where even after getting spanked one night, teams will regularly beat that same opponent on the very next day. The MLB is the best league in the world for a reason — there are no bad players or bad teams.

It would be silly for a professional team to concede defeat, just as it's silly to suggest that players shouldn't be allowed to bunt to break up a no-hitter. You play as hard as you can until the end of the game *because it's your job.*

Lest we forget, it's still possible for a team down 10 runs to win a game. Of course, it's unlikely, but isn't that why we watch sports in the first place — to see unbelievable things happen?

And just to address the pace of play argument, which suggests that the mercy rule could be used as a way to drive down the average MLB game time, I have a few things to say.

1. The number of games that would use the mercy rule and the number of innings that would be skipped wouldn't be enough to cause a significant change in average game time.

2. The solution to improving the pace of play in baseball is not to just play less baseball. That's essentially the same thing as admitting you can't solve the problem, as the actual baseball that gets played will still have the same lethargic pace.

The level of competition in Major League Baseball does not warrant the inclusion of a mercy rule. If teams want to limit pitcher innings by having position players pitch, let them do so. At least fans enjoy the spectacle. If you can keep people tuned into a blowout baseball game, that's a good thing.

SHOULD THE NBA ELIMINATE FOULING OUT?

Originally published: October 25, 2019

With 50 seconds left in the first game of the 2019 NBA Season, New Orleans Pelicans guard J.J. Redick drew a charge against Toronto Raptors forward Pascal Siakam.

That charge marked Siakam's sixth foul, meaning he had fouled out and was no longer eligible to play. Siakam, arguably the best player in the game, had led his team with 34 points and 18 rebounds. But with less than a minute left and the Raptors facing a two-point deficit, his night was over.

Toronto was able to force overtime and win the game, salvaging their opening night. Yet, Siakam's absence stripped us from watching a great player battle in the clutch. SB Nation writer Matt Ellentuck shared his thoughts on the matter, reigniting an interesting debate: should the NBA allow players to foul out of games?

Just two days later, reigning MVP Giannis Antetokounmpo fouled out with five minutes left of the Milwaukee Bucks' season opener against the Houston Rockets. And playing with five fouls down the stretch, James Harden nearly missed the game's final moments himself.

Had the last two NBA MVPs been unavailable for crunch time, it would have been a big disappointment. After all, seeing star players duke it out with the game on the line is a big part of why we watch basketball. So, if we value an entertaining product above all else, it would make sense to eliminate the idea of fouling out.

It's not like this means fouling would go unpunished. Any foul committed would still go down as a team foul, meaning teams would still want to avoid putting their opponents in the bonus, giving them free throws on every foul, shooting or otherwise.

For an example of this, look no further than football. Players can commit an unlimited amount of penalties and remain in the game, but no one intentionally violates the rules because they get penalized for doing so. And players can still receive ejections for committing multiple unsportsmanlike conduct penalties, just as NBA players could still be ejected for technical and flagrant fouls.

Even going back to James Naismith's original rules, players weren't ejected for committing fouls. After a player's second foul, they were just removed from the game until the next goal was scored, effectively leading to an untimed power play for the opposing team. This rule was in place until the invention of the free throw.

That being said, there are reasons why this wouldn't be the best idea. For one, it would enable players to use the "Hack-a-Shaq" strategy more often against poor foul shooters.

While this is a valid tactic, and players who struggled heavily from the line deserve to have their weakness exploited, this would only lead to more free throws, the slowest and least interesting part of the game. Free throws aren't good entertainment, so allowing players to comfortably foul liabilities from the charity stripe without risking foul trouble could backfire.

Eliminating fouling out would also eliminate many of the strategic decisions surrounding players in foul trouble. Coaches would no longer have to make the call on whether to leave players on the court, risking them picking up additional fouls or sit them on the bench, potentially putting their team at a disadvantage. Similarly, teams would no longer be able to attack defending players in foul trouble with the goal of drawing another foul on them.

And finally, there is certainly something to be said for disincentivizing fouling as a whole in order to keep the game safe and civil. With no risk of fouling out, players may be more inclined to foul opponents as means of retribution for hard fouls on themselves, which could make the game more violent and less about the actual basketball.

Upon weighing both the pros and cons, I don't think the NBA should keep its rule disqualifying players following their sixth personal foul. Sure, this might lessen the excitement of some late-game scenarios, but the fault is on the player for fouling out in the first place.

However, I do think the NBA should consider allowing players a seventh personal foul for games that go into overtime. It makes no sense for players to be held to the same foul restrictions in games that go longer than anticipated. Games that require multiple overtimes can turn into a war of attrition just to see who can have more of their starters still available.

There are still some questions to consider, such as if players will be given one extra foul for each overtime or just a seventh for the entirety of overtime, and if players who have fouled out will be allowed to return for overtime, but for now, I'll leave those decisions to the league.

SHOULD THE FORMAT OF THE WORLD CHESS CHAMPIONSHIP BE CHANGED?

Originally published: December 3, 2019

On February 10, 1996, the worlds of chess and supercomputing changed forever. In the first game of a highly publicized six-game series, Deep Blue, a chess-playing computer developed by IBM, defeated Garry Kasparov, the reigning world chess champion.

This marked the first time that a computer program beat a chess world champion in a classical game under tournament regulations. Kasparov would rebound to win the match 4–2, but in a May 1997 rematch, Deep Blue emerged victorious 3.5–2.5.

In perhaps the most famous strategy game of them all, machine had bested man.

Deep Blue's triumph marked a turning point in artificial intelligence, suggesting that machines were approaching, and even surpassing human thinking. Since then, computers have only continued learning, and are now capable of beating humans in even more complex games such as Go and poker.

Nowadays, it's safe to say that a human chess player will never reach the level of top chess computers, which are still improving. Players of all skill levels regularly turn to chess engines to study both their own games and databases of recorded games.

The influence of this technology is particularly conspicuous at the top levels of competitive chess. In preparation for tournaments and major events such as the World Chess Championship, players will heavily study the past games and tendencies of their opponents. Often with the aid of "seconds," which are essentially highly-rated assistants, players will attempt to predict opening lines opponents will use and formulate their own strategies.

During broadcasts of last year's World Chess Championship between reigning champion Magnus Carlsen and challenger Fabiano Caruana, commentators analyzed the ongoing Championship matches while simultaneously pulling up previously played games featuring similar situations to those currently taking place. All the while, chess engines evaluated the game after each move, determining which player was in a better situation.

The effect of advancements in chess engines on the modern game is evident. Players now memorize as many openings and variations as possible, with all the computing power and training tools at their disposal. And although this has certainly increased the skill of top players, it hasn't come without a cost. That cost comes in the form of draws.

With higher level study comes higher level play, and as quality rises to new heights, the margins between the best players will become slimmer. And, since most people believe that a game played perfectly by both sides ends in a draw (although chess remains unsolved), this means that over time we should expect to see more draws in top competitions.

This brings us back to the 2018 World Chess Championship. The format used for the match was a best-of-12, where the first player to 6.5 wins. For each game, the players received 100 minutes to act, with an additional 50 minutes after move 40, 15 minutes after move 60, and 30 seconds added on after every individual move. This format is known as classical time control. After at least 30 moves had been made by each side, the players were allowed to mutually agree to a draw at any time.

However, for the first time in World Chess Championship history, all 12 games were drawn, leaving the score at 6–6.

This meant the championship went to tiebreakers, starting with a best-of-four "rapid" games, with 25 minutes for each side and an additional 10 seconds after each move. If the match had remained tied, progressively quicker tiebreakers would have been used, ending with a sudden-death match where the player with white pieces receives more time, but a draw counts as a win for black.

However, that wasn't necessary. Carlsen won each of the first three rapid games, ending the series and retaining his title. It wasn't the first time Carlsen was forced to tiebreakers. His previous title defense in 2016 against Sergey Karjakin went to rapid games after both players won a game apiece with the other 10 drawn.

In fact, it seemed Carlsen was more than happy to take the match to tiebreakers in 2018. Despite holding a better position after 30 moves in the 12th game, Carlsen offered a surprising draw, preferring his odds in the tiebreak games.

Carlsen's decision paid off and was likely the right decision, but it was poorly received and no doubt bad for competitive chess. Intentionally playing for a draw is arguably against the spirit of the game and will only harm fan interest in these elite competitions.

Since the World Chess Championship moved to 12-game, champion vs. challenger format in 2008, 75% of games using classical time control have ended in draws. Over the last two matches in 2016 and 2018, that number rises to above 90%.

As standalone games, many of the draws haven't been "boring," but that's not what matters. When the perception is that every game is a draw, which changes nothing in the course of a series, there is little reason for people to pay attention.

Given that draws are occurring so frequently, that we shouldn't expect this trend to reverse course, and that playing for tie-breakers has become a viable strategy, it might be time to question the method used to determine a world champion.

Should the format of the World Chess Championship be changed?

Full disclosure — I'm by no means a chess expert — I know how to play, and I play on occasion, but that's about as far as my chess proficiency goes.

I am, however, someone very interested in the structure of sports and competitions in general, and someone who believes we should always be willing to examine our rules and change them if doing so would lead to a better overall contest.

This can be defined in many different ways, including to make a competition fairer or more entertaining. I believe the World Chess Championship is currently failing to meet its original purposes, and because of this, we should consider changing it.

Private matches arranged between top players for the proclaimed title of world champion have occurred since the mid-19th century. Formal systems for determining the best in the world have existed since 1948.

Over time, the specifics have changed. At some points, there have been one-on-one matches. At other times, there have been tournaments. The number of games played in a match has fluctuated. So, too, has the time control.

But while the details may not have always been consistent, the concept has — the World Chess Championship exists to showcase the highest-level chess on earth and determine a clear world champion. In practice, this means to find the best chess players, have them play enough games to generate a worthy sample size, and give them a reasonable amount of time to play these games so they can perform at or near their best.

These are good objectives. Upon closer examination, though, the World Chess Championship does not achieve them.

For most of chess history, it was assumed that the best player in the world would be a human. Deep Blue's victory over Garry Kasparov in 1997 forever changed that view. For a few years following that match, it may have been unclear whether man or machine was better, but by now, it has been long established that computers are highly superior.

In terms of determining a clear world champion, the World Chess Championship also struggles. Three of the last five championship matches have gone to tiebreakers, and in 2018, not a single decisive result was reached under classical time control. It is now more common than not to determine the chess world champion through rapid chess, a format with its own world championship entirely.

So, if the World Chess Championship does not crown the best chess-playing entity, and is inefficient in determining even the best human player, why wouldn't we want to change it?

Let's evaluate some potential changes. My goal here isn't to advocate for anything in particular, but to open a discussion of both changes and the factors which should go into the decision-making process.

My first instinct was to look at time control, specifically reducing the time players have to make their moves. The more time players are allotted, the more considered and ultimately better their moves can be. It then follows that forcing them to make quicker decisions will lead to more variance and fewer draws.

So, what would the optimal time control be? Unfortunately, there is no easy solution, as this question forces us to rethink what we want from the World Chess Championship.

If that answer is entertainment, to improve the spectator experience and increase fan viewership, then it would make sense to use extremely tight time control.

In recent years, blitz and bullet chess (even quicker than blitz, often allowing each player only one minute for the entire game) have become very popular online for their intense pace and accommodating nature. Not everyone can set aside an hour to play a match, but anyone can find a few minutes to get their fix.

Some of the most exciting chess I've seen has come from watching online bullet tournaments. Even though I don't understand everything that's happening, it all moves at such a breathtaking speed that it's almost impossible to look away.

If the World Chess Championship was played in a bullet format, you could play 100 games within the same time it currently takes to play just one classic game. There would be non-stop action, and such a high sample size of games would almost definitely lead to a clear victor emerging.

That might all be true, but it would still be a terrible idea. The best chess players in the world may be computers, but the World Chess Championship should still strive to determine the best human player. Doing so with a series of one-minute games would be a farce.

Preparation for a match would involve getting used to the time control more than anything else, and it makes studying advanced tactics and endgames, in particular, meaningless because there will never be enough time to put concepts into action. It would teach young and recreational players to exclusively play bullet when no person can become great at chess through lightning-quick games alone.

Even from a viewing perspective, bullet games don't leave enough time for commentators to teach or explain the players' thought processes. Most important of all, a winner would, in all likelihood, be established early on in the match, as there is a greater variation in the abilities of players as matches get faster.

Let's not forget that Magnus Carlsen intentionally took his match with Fabiano Caruana to tiebreakers, even when he held a better position in the 12th game. That was just to reach a four-game match of rapid games. Can you imagine how excited he would have been to play Caruana in 100 bullet games? Surely, the match would lose all interest once Carlsen took a significant lead.

Subverting the game for entertainment purposes makes no sense — after all, chess isn't supposed to be a spectator sport. However, we can't ignore these interests, either. Some people believe the solution is to extend the championship match to 16 or even 24 games, as it has been in the past.

The additional games might give players more freedom to experiment, but for the very same reason that each individual game is less important, public interest in the event could wane. At some point, the match becomes too long to hold people's attention, and it could even be putting too much on the players themselves.

As much as chess wishes money wasn't a factor, without sponsors and media coverage, major events wouldn't exist, or at least not on the scale they currently do. Chess owes a lot to its marketable personalities such as Garry Kasparov and Magnus Carlsen.

Playing bullet in the Chess World Championship obviously makes no sense. Rapid and blitz are equally poor options, not least because world championships for these time controls already exist.

Perhaps a better option would be to reduce the current amount of time given to players by a third or a half, shortening games while still allowing plenty of time to think and play high-quality chess. It's unclear how significantly this would affect the frequency of draws in championship matches or public interest as a whole.

Would people even notice the difference between very long and just long games of chess? I'm not sure, but it's something that could be looked into.

The concept of chess becoming stale due to a "draw death" as players improve and begin to draw more and more of their games is not a new one. Over time, several top players have proposed modifications to the game to combat draw death. Former world champions José Raúl Capablanca and Bobby Fischer have even created entirely new variants of chess.

Fischer's version, the more popular of the two, was announced in 1996 as Fischer Random and is also known as Chess960. The game plays exactly like chess, except with the position of players' home rank pieces (the backline of pieces behind the pawns) randomized. With only a few restrictions on the otherwise randomized order, the "960" refers to the number of possible starting positions.

Fischer Random makes the heavy study of openings found in traditional chess impractical, as there are far too many starting positions to memorize and very limited research has been done on each specific position. This makes Fischer Random more about a player's raw talent and ability to think creatively in unique situations.

Because of these factors, Fischer Random is one of the more appealing chess variants. In fact, the International Chess Federation (FIDE) recently held the first World Fischer Random Chess Championship.

However, because similarly to blitz and bullet chess, there isn't much value in studying the game, Fischer Random's value in terms of competitive play seems limited. It will remain popular, but likely never overtake traditional chess.

Neither will Capablanca Chess, which dates back to the 1920s and features an 8x10 chessboard with two new pieces: the archbishop, with powers of both a bishop and a knight, and the chancellor, which can act as both a rook and knight.

Although Capablanca Chess succeeds in both creating a more complex game and one that with defined pieces and no specific time control can be seriously studied, the fact that this version of chess is played on a different board and with different pieces makes it inaccessible to most, and ultimately a tough sell.

There are many different variants to chess, including Seirawan Chess, Four-player Chess, Losing Chess, and others, but while they are worth experimenting with, the future of the Chess World Championship does not lay with a game merely similar to chess.

Perhaps the way forward isn't with a head-to-head match in the first place, but rather a tournament. As recently as 2007, the world champion was decided through an eight-person, double round-robin tournament. A Candidates Tournament is still used to determine the challenger for the Chess World Championship.

Tournaments are seen as better for risk-taking, as unlike a head-to-head match, where a player can't lose unless they lose an individual game, draws alone won't cut it in a tournament. Once one player has won a game, anyone else looking to compete for the championship has to match it.

Because you don't have total control over your fate, aggression is encouraged, which, in theory, leads to fewer draws. You can't play to not lose — you have to play to win.

Perhaps draws could be disincentivized even further by adopting the soccer-style scoring system which gives three points for a win and one for a draw, rather than chess' current format of one point for a win and one-half point for a draw.

With three points for a win, a player with one victory and two defeats and a player with three draws would each have three points. It would certainly be a game-changer, although there could be a contentious debate over the fairness of this scoring format.

There is also the question of whether or not the reigning champion should be given an advantage in this tournament. Before tiebreakers were used, it was traditionally the case that the reigning world champion would keep his title if the match ended in a draw. Emanuel Lasker once even proposed to Capablanca that he should remain world champion unless Capablanca could beat him by two games.

If the Chess World Championship were to move to a tournament format, would it make sense to give the reigning champion an advantage, perhaps starting with the equivalent of one win? Should they be declared champions in the event of a tie? I don't think so — a world champion should have to prove that they are indeed the best in the world. However, other people may have differing views.

Finally, there are additional modifications to scoring that could be considered. The first of these would be to, in the case of draws, award a win, or perhaps .75 points to .25, to the player with more time remaining.

I have seen this suggested, although it seems to be flawed for a few reasons. Naturally, this would eliminate draw offers, as players behind on time would never agree to a loss. Instead, it could lead to desperate plays and aesthetically displeasing scenarios where players pointlessly move their pieces about until the 50-Move Rule ends the game.

It also seems unfair, particularly when draws are so common, to establish rules permitting players a certain amount of time to act and then subsequently penalizing them for using that time. This rule would unintentionally lead to games of speed chess with each player's main objective being to play as fast as possible in a way that avoids a checkmate.

A much more reasonable suggestion would be to award .75 points to a player who puts their opponent into a stalemate, and .25 points for the player who is stalemated. Currently, stalemates count as draws for each side, but some, including Lasker, believe that a player should be penalized for being unable to move their king. Changing the way some draws are scored in competitive matches would open up new strategies and reduce the chances of matches ending in ties.

There are certainly more possibilities to be considered, but these represent many of the more commonly discussed solutions to drawing in chess. It remains up for debate how large of an issue drawing is at the Chess World Championships and other major tournaments. It might not be huge at the moment, but if current trends continue over the next few years, it'll become a much larger talking point.

The concept of draw death is an interesting one. While computers plug away at improving and solving chess with no end in sight, it's safe to say we won't be able to achieve perfect play. However, as we reach the upper limits of human chess potential, the very top talents could reach something of a stalemate.

THE BEST COLLEGE FOOTBALL PLAYOFF FORMAT

Originally published: December 15, 2019

It seems every year since the College Football Playoff was established in 2014, there has been chatter about potential playoff expansion and debate over what the best playoff format would be.

With this year's CFP just a few weeks away, the conversation was reignited again by a report suggesting that an eight-team format featuring the Power 5 champions, the highest-finishing Group of 5 team, and two at-large bids is gaining traction among the powers that be.

This model has certainly been the most popular one I've seen passed around, with its proponents claiming it to be the fairest proposal. The winner of each conference gets a guaranteed spot, while also giving a Group of 5 team a chance to make some noise and allowing two at-large slots for independents like Notre Dame or worthy teams that failed to win their conference.

Under this proposal, everyone gets an opportunity. My question is: should they? I believe a different eight-team format would be best for the College Football Playoff. But first, let's discuss a few of the more general questions surrounding expansion.

When would a potential expansion take place?

Any CFP expansion would go into effect two years after its announcement. In theory, this means the earliest possible time we could see an expanded playoff would be for the 2022 season.

However, most people in the college football community seem pleased with the current system. At the very least, there is no urgent need to usher in change. Doing so now likely wouldn't even be possible, as there are still many aspects that would need to be worked out.

Far and away, the likeliest time for a change would be the 2026 season, the first year of the CFP's next television deal. The current contract, signed with ESPN, began along with the start of the CFP in 2014 and runs for 12 years, through the end of the 2025 season.

Both sides seem content to let the contract play out. As we get deeper into the deal, negotiations for the following deal will take place. Playoff expansion is likely to factor heavily into those talks.

Is eight the right number of teams for the CFP?

I think so. The current format is the best system college football has put in place for determining a national champion so far. It still blows my mind that there wasn't even a real championship game until the 1990s.

Sure, there will be some years like 2018 where two teams are clearly better than the rest of the field and dominate their semifinal matchups (the same could be true for 2019 with LSU and Ohio State, but that remains to be seen).

But far more often, there is a real debate surrounding who deserves to play for a national championship, particularly in years where there are three undefeated teams. Clemson may only be ranked #3 this season, but they are the defending national champions and have won all 13 of their games by an average of 36 points. Leaving them out doesn't make sense. Nor does having everything decided by a computer. The switch to a four-team playoff with teams chosen by a selection committee is a big step for college football.

This doesn't mean the system is perfect, though. Under the current format, half of FBS schools begin the season with no chance to compete for the title. While every FBS team is eligible for the CFP, in reality, only Power 5 schools and Notre Dame stand a chance at competing.

We knew this going in, but luckily, UCF was able to demonstrate this fact during the 2017 and 2018 seasons. In 2017, the Knights finished just 12th in the final CFP rankings despite being the only undefeated FBS team. They won their bowl game against Auburn to cap off a perfect year.

Then, the following season, they went undefeated yet again through their conference championship game. Still, UCF finished just #8 in that year's CFP rankings, still some distance away from the top four. If a team can go undefeated in back-to-back seasons and still not receive playoff consideration, they never stood a chance at all.

Expansion to an eight-team playoff still wouldn't guarantee teams like UCF a spot in the field, but the opportunity would still exist. And with a field that size, I think the committee would be more willing to give Power 5 teams a chance. As much as I would love to guarantee a spot to any undefeated teams, that would only incentivize weak non-conference scheduling, and a 16-team playoff would likely dilute the field too heavily.

So, an eight-team playoff beginning in the 2026 season seems to be a strong possibility. How should we decide which eight teams compete for a title? I don't think the plan of taking the Power 5 champions, one Group of 5 team, and two at-larges is poor, but we can do better.

I don't think we should guarantee any teams a spot in the field of eight. Instead, a committee should simply choose and rank who they believe to be the top eight teams in the country. It's that simple, and it would lead to the most competitive games.

While guaranteeing a Group of 5 team a spot would all but solve the UCF problem, it's also true that the Group of 5 may not always be worthy of a spot in the field. #17 Memphis had a great season and finished as the highest-ranked Group of 5 team, but I don't think they'd be in my top eight.

In the same regard, Power 5 champions may not necessarily be deserving of a spot. Last year, a 10–3 Washington team won the Pac-12 and finished #9 in the CFP rankings. I'd have taken UCF over them, which would leave the Huskies on the outside looking in.

Just think about if Virginia had somehow managed to beat Clemson in the ACC Championship this year. The Cavaliers would be given an automatic spot in the field, even though they probably wouldn't be deserving of one. That might knock out a team like Baylor who finished #7, only losing two games by a combined 10 points to Oklahoma.

Perhaps what frustrates me the most about the leading expansion proposal is that it assumes the ACC, Big 10, Big 12, Pac-12, and SEC are and will always be the best conferences in college football. If we're being honest, the American might be better than the ACC and Pac-12 right now. It's better than the Pac-12 in basketball, too.

This shouldn't be a huge surprise. The American was founded by members of the old Big East, which was a power conference. Who's to say another round of realignment won't cripple a league like the Big 12? It makes no sense to force the American to compete with four other conferences for one spot when they have much more in common with the Power 5 than, for instance, the MAC.

As we transition to the second half of ESPN's CFP rights deal, eight-team expansion seems like the way to go for the future. However, there are still many things to be decided, such as how to determine which teams make the field, where the quarterfinal games will be played, and if any additional schedule changes need to be made to accommodate the extra games.

For my money, though, the plan that makes the most sense isn't to divvy up spots by conference, but rather by giving the best eight teams a chance to win it all.

V: BEST OF THE REST

COLLEGE BASKETBALL OVERVALUES MARCH MADNESS RESULTS

Originally published: May 4, 2019

As the spring semester starts to wind down at most schools across the United States, it also brings an end to the frantic period of colleges introducing their new head coaches and finalizing their recruiting classes.

Expectations are on everyone's mind during the offseason and no team faces higher standards than Duke. Coach K's Blue Devils, coming off a season where they entered the NCAA Tournament as the #1 overall seed and reached the Elite Eight, have secured their fourth-straight top-ranked recruiting class.

Led by returning point guard Tre Jones and three five-star recruits, Duke is poised to be highly competitive once again, something that has not gone unnoticed by media outlets. However, are the expectations for this program too high? I've seen many comments arguing that despite all of their talent, Duke won't even win the National Championship next year, to which my natural reaction is, "well yeah, probably".

This got me to thinking: if the main barometer of success for major college basketball programs is their March Madness results (specifically, their number of Final Fours and titles), then we are severely overlooking regular season success in favor of a notoriously unpredictable tournament.

It's not hard to understand why we do this. March Madness is the ultimate money maker. Advancing in the tournament provides schools with a higher proportion of revenues, along with national attention and a boost to future recruiting. Coaches can earn huge bonuses (Virginia's Tony Bennett earned $1.25 million over the course of this year's tournament) and use a strong showing to garner attention for bigger jobs. You can be successful in the regular season, but March Madness is where winning gets noticed.

Especially following their loss to 16-seed UMBC in the 2018 tournament, the Virginia Cavaliers were considered tournament underachievers. Now with a title under their belts, that will no longer be the case. And despite making March Madness every year since Mark Few took over in 1999–00, many thought Gonzaga was incapable of contending for a title until they did just that, reaching the championship game in 2017.

Like Virginia and Gonzaga, Duke is another team whose tournament success is under constant scrutiny. Critics will be quick to point out that the Blue Devils have made just two Final Fours over the past 15 years. Disregarding the fact that those were both National Championships, and that extending to the past 20 years, Duke has two additional Final Fours and a third title (can you tell I'm not buying this argument?), how big an underachievement could two Final Fours in 15 years really be?

Only 15 of over 350 Division I schools have made multiple Final Fours over the last 15 years. Less than 10% of schools (31) have made even one. While Duke does trail blue bloods like Michigan State and North Carolina (who lead the way with 5), Kentucky (4), and Kansas (3), I would argue this level of success is extremely hard to maintain over time. For example, UCLA and Indiana, who have a combined 16 championships, have not made the Final Four since 2008 and 2002, respectively. If repeated tournament success is so difficult, why not focus on something equally difficult but more controllable and arguably more impressive: regular season dominance?

Yet, tons of teams enter every season with Final Four aspirations, leading to inevitable disappointment. It's not like we can blame them — you dream of championships, not 20, 25, 30-win seasons. But those title visions can neglect real achievement. Contrary to many, I don't think Duke underperformed this past season. I understand the championship or bust mentality, especially considering how the team featured the top three overall recruits and were already being talked about before the season as one of the potentially greatest teams ever, but let's bring ourselves back down to reality.

Duke was the #1 overall seed in the tournament. That means entering March Madness, they were deemed the best team in the country. How can that be a disappointment? Yet, they still lost five games during the regular season, a testament to how difficult it is to go undefeated in today's college basketball.

In the last 40 seasons, only three teams have entered March Madness undefeated. The last undefeated champion was Indiana, who finished 32–0 in 1976. It's worth noting that now, an undefeated season requires a team to win around 40 games.

Entering March Madness, Duke had an overall record of 29–5, good for a win rate of .853. Using the tournament as a pure extension of the regular season, a team that wins 85.3% of their games has only a 52.9% chance of winning four in a row, which would get them to the Final Four. That's basically a coin flip, without even considering that the average March Madness game is tougher than Duke's average regular season game, even in a conference as strong as the ACC. Historically, #1 seeds have made the Final Four just over 40% of the time.

A single-elimination tournament, while adding intensity and excitement to each match, also increases variance tremendously. There's a reason why major upsets rarely occur in the

NBA Playoffs. The seven-game series is not designed for the underdog. Anyone can beat a team once, but four times? It would be very difficult to argue March Madness has been bad for college basketball, but by inviting chaos, you decrease the chance of the best team coming out on top.

As long as we acknowledge the inherent randomness of the NCAA Tournament and that teams can advance further than superior teams (after all, that's what upsets are — no one actually thinks 2018 UMBC was a better team than 2018 Virginia), we'll be fine. The unpredictability of March Madness is a big part of why it's so great. Let's just not let one bad performance tell the story of a team's season when their first 30+ games do a much better job.

THE MEDIA TEST THAT DEFINES THE GREATEST TEAM SPORT ATHLETES

Originally published: May 9, 2019

An athlete's legacy can be largely shaped by how they are treated by the media. Because of this, LeBron James, Lionel Messi, and Cristiano Ronaldo will be remembered as the greatest team sport athletes of this generation. A few other stars can be argued, but two moments from this past week show why these three names stand alone.

The first comes from Game 3 of the NBA Western Conference Semifinals series between the Golden State Warriors and Houston Rockets. With just 50 seconds remaining, the Warriors trail 110–109 with the ball. Clint Capela has been switched on to Kevin Durant on the perimeter, providing an ideal matchup for the former MVP.

As Durant begins to drive, P.J. Tucker is positioned in the middle of the paint to provide help defense. Durant then swings the ball to a wide-open Andre Iguodala in the corner who buries a three, giving the Warriors a two-point lead as a signature "BANG!" call from Mike Breen sounds through millions of televisions.

During the subsequent overtime period, Mark Jackson reflected on the play, noting the difference in reaction if LeBron James had made the same decision as Durant.

"…With 41 points, Kevin Durant, instead of shooting the rock, when it mattered most, made the right play to a wide-open Andre Iguodala. If that's LeBron James, they call that deferring, and they're upset."

He's absolutely right.

The second moment came in the aftermath of the second leg of the UEFA Champions League semifinals between FC Barcelona and Liverpool. Barcelona took a 3–0 lead into Anfield after a dominant performance in the first leg from Lionel Messi, their star player and a man locked in perpetual competition with Cristiano Ronaldo for the title of the greatest player in the world and perhaps the greatest of all-time.

Messi knocked in two goals during that first-leg match, including a stunning free kick that marked his 600th goal for Barcelona. After the game, all anyone could talk about was Messi's brilliance, and how blessed we are to be alive in a time where we can witness this legend with our own eyes.

Fast-forward to the reverse fixture, and Liverpool pulls off the unthinkable, outhustling and outmuscling an unprepared Barcelona side to the tune of a 4–0 victory, sending the Reds through to the final 4–3 on aggregate in one of the most stunning comebacks in Champions League history.

Just as quickly as the tide turned in Liverpool's favor, all the admiration sent Messi's way turned into criticism, labeling him as a choker and someone who fails to show up for the biggest games. Calls of "he'll never be the greatest" and "where is your GOAT now?" were all too common.

The same holds true for Ronaldo. Whenever he turns in a great performance, we've never seen anything like it. Get knocked out of a tournament, and he's overrated.

These examples show a unique responsibility placed on LeBron,

Messi, and Ronaldo for every element of their team's successes and failures. No other players are treated quite the same. Every win or loss is presented as a direct reflection of their quality as a player.

LeBron's expectations are clear — to compete for and win a championship every season. No player in NBA history has had a greater singular impact on his team than LeBron.

In the 2009–10 season, LeBron's Cavaliers went 61–21, finishing first place in the Eastern Conference. That summer, LeBron joined the Heat during free agency. The following season, the Cavs finished 19–63, last place in the East and a full 42 games worse than the previous season. In total, during the three seasons following LeBron switching teams, his former team finished with a record 90 games worse than they had with LeBron the year before. On average, that is a staggering difference of 30 wins with LeBron versus without him. For eight straight seasons from 2011–18, his team made the NBA Finals.

Perhaps LeBron's greatest career accomplishment came in the 2016 NBA Finals when in his second year back in Cleveland and a rematch of the previous year's finals, he gave the city its first championship in over 50 years by defeating a Warriors team which had set a new NBA record with 73 regular-season victories. For many, this title pushed him over the edge, past Michael Jordan.

But what happened in the next two years? Once again, James found himself matched up against a favored Warriors team, now armed with a fourth All-Star and second former MVP, Kevin Durant. Despite herculean efforts, the Warriors won both series — 2017 in five games, and 2018 in just four.

LeBron failed.

Never mind that he averaged a 33-point triple-double in the 2017 series, an astonishing feat. Disregard that he nearly did the same thing in 2018, averaging 34 points, 8.5 rebounds, and 10 assists. Forget that following the 2017 Finals, Kyrie Irving, LeBron's sidekick for the past three years, requested a trade and became a member of the Celtics. The 2018 Cavaliers had absolutely no business making the finals, yet they did just that, winning game 7 in Boston against Irving's Celtics to clinch their spot. They were a historically weak NBA Finals team with three fewer All-Stars than their opponent, being carried by one man. But none of that mattered.

LeBron failed.

When you are a player of that caliber and lose, individual performance is disregarded. In the 2015 Finals, the first of the four-straight Warriors-Cavs matchups, Andre Iguodala was awarded Finals MVP, largely for being the primary defender on LeBron James. LeBron still averaged 35.8 points, 13.3 rebounds, and 8.8 assists. When you are so good that the player that guards you in a series gets MVP despite your superhuman performance, just because you lost the series, failure is not an option.

Sometimes, even your successes are viewed as failures. LeBron is often criticized for his finals record, which currently stands at 3–6. It certainly doesn't help that Jordan went 6–0 in his finals appearances. But Jordan was also favored every time, while James was the underdog in seven of his nine trips, almost always going up against the Spurs and Warriors dynasties.

It makes no sense to use NBA Finals losses (or losses in any championship) as an attack on someone's resume. Reaching the finals is a huge achievement. To have a 3–6 finals record, one has to make the finals NINE times.

But for people like LeBron, making the Finals isn't enough. You have to win, and you are expected to do everything, even if that might be to the detriment of your team.

This leads me back to Mark Jackson's comments on Kevin Durant's assist to Andre Iguodala. So much of the story is unfortunately told by results-oriented thinking, but if LeBron makes that pass and his teammate misses the shot, everyone questions why LeBron didn't shoot himself.

In the clutch, stars are supposed to take matters into their own hands, even though that might not be the best decision. That's just how it goes. The best end up getting blamed for things that aren't their fault.

Lionel Messi knows this all too well. After seeing the reaction to Barcelona's 4–0 loss at Liverpool, it seems only reasonable to ask everyone making Messi jokes one question: "Do you know what position he plays?"

As a center forward, Messi bears about as much responsibility for allowing Liverpool's four goals as Marc-André ter Stegen, Barcelona's goalkeeper, has credit for Messi's two goals in the first leg.

Sure, Messi didn't have a magical moment in the second leg, but he was still able to create a few strong chances and was one of Barcelona's best players in the match. Barca's defenders, on the other hand, were simply outclassed and lacked composure.

Of course, Messi could've sent Barcelona through to the Champions League Final with just one goal. He certainly could've done more. But since matches are scored on aggregate, the second leg is effectively an extension of the first. Two goals over two games is not an underperformance. Once again, there are examples of this with Ronaldo as well — we're just in the Messi cycle right now.

All of this comes down to the fact that LeBron, Messi, and Ronaldo have extreme, and perhaps unfair expectations placed on them every time they play. No other team sport athlete faces the same kind of pressure, and because of the way we treat them, they will go down as the greatest team sport athletes of this era.

It doesn't matter if Kevin Durant ends his career with better numbers or more rings. Durant will never have the same individual responsibility as LeBron James. If the Warriors fail to win the title this season, it will be deemed a failure for the Warriors, not KD. (Ignore Durant's injury last night — this has been the case for the last several seasons, even going back to his Thunder years.)

So why are these three players viewed differently, even when compared to similarly great players in other sports? I think a big part comes down to the ongoing storyline of the GOAT quest. For essentially the last decade, LeBron has been competing to surpass Jordan, and Messi and Ronaldo have gone back and forth one-upping each other.

When you're trying to be the greatest ever, the stakes are naturally raised. Every win helps the case, every loss harms it, and every performance that isn't spectacular has to be a choke.

This isn't the case with Tom Brady. At this stage, most people wouldn't have a problem with calling Brady the greatest quarterback of all-time. No other quarterback or team has had the sustained dominance of Brady and the Patriots over the last two decades. But even among those who would argue another name, there isn't a consensus as to who that player is. Joe Montana? Peyton Manning? Aaron Rodgers? The competition is unclear, so Brady is solidified at the top.

Another person that comes to mind is Lee Sang-Hyeok, aka "Faker". The SK Telecom T1 (SKT) star mid laner led his team to League of Legends World Championships in 2013, 2015, and 2016, and became widely considered the best player in the history of the game.

In the 2017 World Championships, SKT struggled but still managed to reach the finals, led by incredible performances from

Faker. However, in the finals against fellow Korean team Samsung Galaxy, SKT's luck ran out, and the three-time champs were swept 3–0.

It's nearly the same story as the 2018 Cleveland Cavaliers, except this time, the reaction was different. SKT teammates were criticized for letting down Faker. It's easier to appreciate greatness for what it is when there isn't anyone to compare it to.

LeBron, Messi, and Ronaldo may very well be the three greatest team sport athletes of their generation, but even if others are right up there, no one else truly understands what it feels like to be them. They had no say in it — the rapid swings in reception come from us trying to make a story.

My advice? If you want to argue GOATs, wait until after those in the conversation retire. Getting hung up on who's better than who only takes away from the brilliance on display.

HATE FOR THE WNBA AND OTHER EMERGING LEAGUES MAKES NO SENSE

Originally published: May 15, 2019

Fans are never satisfied with the breakdown of sports media coverage. People will complain about LeBron James and Zion Williamson being shoved in their faces, but whenever outlets feature less popular or emerging sports, their tune changes to some variant of "who cares?" or "stick to real sports."

I've always found this apparent hypocrisy to be an interesting consequence of the social media age, where everyone feels emboldened to share their opinions concerning just about anything. In actuality, it's probably not as much hypocrisy as it is a combination of different groups of people reacting to different articles and our online tendency to spin things in negative ways.

What this does prove is that people have different tastes, which by itself should demonstrate that we should have coverage of a wide variety of sports and athletes. Yet, the dissatisfaction continues.

I understand it can sometimes feel annoying to be bombarded with irrelevant details of LeBron's offseason actions, but I've never quite gotten why some like to hate on less popular sports and their athletes.

Perhaps no league has had to deal with more of this behavior than the WNBA, which is routinely mocked for its low attendance numbers (although they outpace the NBA at the same point in its history) and "boring" product, among other things. When the league's low salaries are brought up, haters become economists, citing how low demand suggests the players don't deserve better compensation.

I've written in much greater detail about the WNBA's past, present, and future, but to summarize my main thoughts, the WNBA is far from an uninteresting league. It's main problems stem from its relative infancy as a league and a lack of visibility in terms of media coverage and the marketing of its star players. Opportunity for growth exists and is aided by a summer regular season where there is little competition with other domestic sports. No one is expecting salaries to equal that of the NBA, but the players should make more, and foreign leagues prove that they can.

Ignoring the sexist undertones specific to many anti-WNBA arguments, the suggestion that less popular leagues don't deserve coverage or higher player salaries is borderline offensive and straight-up anti-progress. Under this line of thinking, nothing should be any more popular than it currently is, leading to perfect maintenance of the status quo.

But, of course, nothing starts out popular. Growth takes time, and just because something is difficult doesn't mean we shouldn't do it, or that we don't have an obligation to try. The only way we improve as a society is through continuing to strive for improvement towards ideals.

Should female basketball players have the same opportunity to play professionally in the United States as males and capitalize financially during their limited time as an athlete? Of course. And the same goes for participants in the next big sport we haven't heard of yet.

Additionally, in 2019, with the entire world at our fingertips, finding content for your favorite sport shouldn't be an issue. I would be somewhat more sympathetic to those who complain about less-popular sports if there were fewer mediums to access information.

In the past, people got their news primarily from newspapers. If you were a fan of basketball in its earliest years, but the local paper only focused on baseball and boxing, you would be understandably frustrated. But now, as long as you have an internet connection, accessibility is not an issue. You have the freedom to choose which websites to follow and authors to read. If you don't like a source, go somewhere else.

Lastly, if you're a sports fan, you should want the sports industry to grow. Emerging sports can introduce innovative ideas and add more energy and resources to the industry. And just think, if no one else cared about the sports you follow, they would cease to exist. So why attack other sports? It only looks bad on sports fans as a whole.

There isn't anyone forcing you to love every sport. If something's boring, don't watch it, just like you don't watch 99% of the things on television. Sport exclusivity — the idea that some sports are worthy of being covered while others aren't — is a foolish and self-centered opinion. Continue to like what you like and scroll through the rest.

Author's Note: Congrats to the WNBA players' union on the new collective bargaining agreement!

WANT TO LEARN MORE ABOUT SPORTS? PLAY MORE VIDEO GAMES.

Originally published: June 12, 2019

I have something of a confession to make. Watching the Stanley Cup Finals, I can't help but feel guilty. I know practically nothing about either team and cheer for the Blues simply because the city of Boston wins too many championships.

Now, there are a lot of people like me who watch hockey exclusively during the NHL Playoffs. Playoff hockey has a reputation for being great, and it is. But what makes me feel so guilty is that I wasn't always like this.

There was a time when I was a big hockey fan, knew rosters up and down, and followed it just like my favorite sports.

The same is true for a number of sports. My baseball knowledge is severely lacking compared to what it once was. I don't wake up early on Saturday mornings to watch the Premier League anymore, and I hardly ever tune in to NASCAR, when for a period I would have no problems watching drivers race for hours.

It's normal for tastes to change over time, but all of these sports have one thing in common: when I was following them the most, I also played their corresponding video games.

For hockey, that game was NHL 11. It's hard to be a fan of a game played on ice when you grow up around Houston, Texas, a place where it hardly ever snows. Houston doesn't have an NHL team, and hardly anyone in the area follows the sport.

But after playing the game at a Canadian friend's house, I became instantly hooked. Shortly thereafter, I bought NHL 11 for myself and proceeded to play it religiously, learning all the rules, familiarizing myself with the rosters, and picking up strategy.

Around the same time, I started playing FIFA, which took this even further. In just weeks, it seemed like I knew all the players on every big team around the world and could identify their strengths and weaknesses. I understood the different formations and styles teams employed and how the transfer window operates through career mode.

I became a highly competitive FIFA player over the years that followed, with each edition of the series being my #1 most played game through probably FIFA 17. Over the last few years, I haven't played as much, and my knowledge of international soccer has dipped somewhat as a result.

After playing most sports game franchises out there, I'm convinced that video games are one of, if not the best way to become a sports fan in the modern world.

This is primarily because video games encourage the player to learn in order to succeed. To play a sports game well requires knowing the sport well. One must understand tactics and be able to adapt to the specific players they are using as well as the opposition. Better players end up being rewarded, which encourages putting more time into the game which only improves knowledge of the sport.

But it doesn't feel like that. To the one playing the game, they're just having fun. Madden does a great job of this by allowing the player to choose every play they run and make numerous pre-snap adjustments, allowing them to create their own game plan and scheme.

Player rating systems used in games offer highly accurate portrayals of athletes in a way that is easy to understand — numbers. At just a glance, one can evaluate a single player or an entire team.

These video games also offer a variety of different modes to suit each individual person. Play now offers the chance to quickly try out a new team or strategy, or simply have fun and experiment by messing around with sliders.

Career modes allow one the opportunity to take control of their own created player or an entire team for a more in-depth experience. Some of my best gaming memories come from taking League Two teams all the way to the Premier League in FIFA.

Online ranked games capitalize on our desire to compete against others, combining it with the addictive nature of video games to create an atmosphere where players will sink hours upon hours into climbing ranked ladders. There can be negative consequences to this, but it certainly keeps people playing and improving their knowledge.

Finally, there is Ultimate Team, which has revolutionized several sports games, particularly FIFA, in recent years. Ultimate Team is the trading card of the 21st century, giving players the thrill of opening packs, then trading players on the open market and building their dream teams.

Special cards such as improved Team of the Week versions of players are the modern autographed or holographic cards, working to both highlight which players have performed well of late in real-life and keep the game alive with rare, limited-time-only, upgraded collectibles.

In a time when rapid increases in technology use have led to declines in the TV viewership and live attendance of some sports, video games present a unique ability to spark interest in young potential fans. These gamers will be interested in following their favorite players and teams in real life.

It may seem difficult to believe, but I believe the best entry point for many sports is not the sport themselves, but the video games about them. Outside of a Stanley Cup Finals Game 7, my best shot at becoming a big hockey fan again might be to pick the controller back up.

THE MYTH OF TAINTED ACHIEVEMENT

Originally published: June 15, 2019

The 2018–19 NBA season will serve as a reminder of how hard it is to win a championship.

When DeMarcus Cousins signed with the Golden State Warriors during free agency last summer, many jumped to conclusions, ready to declare the Warriors three-peat champions and move on to the next season. After all, Cousins gave the Warriors a starting lineup comprised of five NBA All-Stars and two former MVPs, none of which were over 30. How could you beat a team like that?

And yet, on Thursday, the Toronto Raptors won their first title in franchise history — on the Warriors home floor, no less. They had done the unthinkable.

Toronto finished the regular season with a better record than the Warriors and won both regular-season meetings. Then in the NBA Finals, they beat the defending champs 4–2 (for an overall mark of 6–2 on the year), including a perfect 3–0 on the road at Oracle Arena. All for a team without a single lottery pick on their roster.

Still, because of injuries — particularly to Warriors stars Kevin Durant and Klay Thompson, some will attempt to delegitimize the Raptors' victory by giving it the figurative asterisk, representing that it is unequal to other titles won in the past. They would have you read the list of recent NBA champions like so:

2017 — Golden State Warriors
2018 — Golden State Warriors
2019 — Toronto Raptors*

The Raptors are far from the first team to get this treatment. It seems that any time a team wins while their opponents aren't at full strength or benefit from a missed call by the officials, the asterisk returns to complain about how things are unfair. When the Warriors beat a Cleveland Cavaliers team in 2015 that had an injured Kyrie Irving and Kevin Love, people played the "what if" game, and said it wouldn't count until they beat a healthy finals squad.

This is unfortunate because sometimes, things really are unfair. Take Lance Armstrong's seven consecutive Tour de France titles. Armstrong doped, and following his cheating scandal, his titles were stripped. You could say he was given the asterisk.

But even in a situation like Armstrong's, the asterisk does little. Everyone knows who finished first in those seven years because history remembers winners. No one knows the names of the second-place finishers that would've taken the gold had Armstrong not competed.

Giving the Toronto Raptors' championship an asterisk is childish and neglects the realities of sport. It likens them to cheaters like Armstrong and diminishes the glory they've earned.

The Raptors had no say in the Warriors' injuries. I'm sure that if given the chance, they would have preferred to have gone up against a fully healthy Warriors team. Athletes understand the realities of injuries and that athletes are real people rather than gods to be worshipped or vilified at the viewer's discretion.

Unfortunately, the Warriors were very unlucky with injuries this season, but injuries are a part of the game — an unpredictable element each team must face. The Raptors simply played the team that took the court opposite them.

An NBA championship isn't won in a single series, either. After beating the Orlando Magic in the first round, Toronto faced the Philadelphia 76ers in a grueling seven-game series that gave the eventual champs everything they could handle.

Then, in the Eastern Conference Finals, the Raptors recovered from a 2–0 deficit against the Milwaukee Bucks, the team with the best record in the league, winning four straight to book the franchise's first appearance in the NBA Finals.

When it finally came time to face the Warriors, who were still armed with plenty of talent and had just swept the Portland Trail Blazers, the Raptors used their depth.

While Kawhi Leonard was consistently great, every other member of the rotation stepped up in big ways. Pascal Siakam carried the load in Game 1 with 32 points on an unbelievable 14/17 shooting. He closed the series almost as spectacularly as he started it, with 26 points, 10 rebounds, and a humongous shot with 26 seconds left to help seal Game 6.

Kyle Lowry had one of his best-ever performances in that Game 6 as well, with 11 points in the first few minutes, and 26 overall, with seven rebounds, 10 assists, and three steals to go with it.

Add in Fred VanVleet's clutch shooting and defense on Stephen Curry, Danny Green's six threes in Game 3, Marc Gasol's 20 points in Game 1 and consistent inside presence throughout the series, and Serge Ibaka's efficient jump shot and six blocks in Game 3, and it's clear the best overall team won the series.

And for that, the Raptors deserve to be celebrated. Winning a championship is incredibly difficult and can never be taken for granted. You can find a way to delegitimize every winner if you look hard enough, but that ultimately changes nothing. So, accept the Raptors as the rightful 2019 NBA Champions. After all, they'll be remembered as such.

THE BURDEN OF INFORMATION: WHY SOME SPORTS ARE MORE POPULAR THAN OTHERS

Originally published: August 15, 2019

In the 21st century, we've reached a time when access to sport, while still not perfect, has expanded to the point where youth can choose to play a variety of different sports.

Television and the media have rapidly increased coverage of sports as a whole and the Olympic movement has provided a regular, global audience to emerging and niche sports, in addition to the traditional mainstays.

Yet, throughout society, and particularly at the professional level, it's obvious that the popularity of individual sports is uneven. In the United States, three sports: football, basketball, and baseball have long dominated the landscape.

It's a fact that goes relatively unquestioned. Although you will sometimes see hockey added to form a "Big 4" or talk of the growth of soccer, there is little doubt that football, basketball, and baseball drive the American sports machine. Some others show up during an important event, or when something amazing happens, while others seem to be shut out entirely.

Of course, it's only natural for some sports to be more popular than others — to have more fans, participants, TV viewership, etc.

But why these three sports in particular?

One answer, and certainly one with a large degree of truth, is simply historical longevity. Sports that have been around for longer have had more opportunity to grow their fanbases, develop and perfect their rules, and achieve financial stability and a degree of legitimacy.

People are more likely to follow sports they grew up playing and watching and enroll their children in them down the line. The NFL is currently celebrating its 100th season, while professional baseball has been around since the 1870s, with the game being played even before that. These sports are ancient.

Basketball is relatively younger, with its major growth taking place in the last half-century. This explains why basketball fans are younger, and the sport has been somewhat of a late addition to the group of powerhouses. It also lends credence to the longevity theory, as it took time for it to become as culturally dominant as it is.

There's more to it than just longevity, though. If there wasn't, we'd see ritualistic games dating back thousands of years taking the center stage. I think there's another reason why certain sports become popular in the first place and continue to draw new fans as generations go by — one that has to do with numbers.

Sports and numbers have an interdependence that goes far beyond the tallies on a scoreboard. Part of the mass appeal of sports is the multitude of ways the actions players perform can be tracked and analyzed, all of which require large volumes of statistics.

Particular in our modern analytics revolution, we look for every single possible aspect of a sport to be analyzed and charted, with teams employing analytics specialists to find any possible edge over their opponents.

Football, basketball, and baseball already had a large number of statistics. For example, quarterbacks were charted by passing yards, passer rating, touchdowns, interceptions, completion percentage, yards per attempt, etc. Now we can measure these things with different personnel groupings against specific defensive formations, at certain times of the game, at different places on the field, depending on how much time they had in the pocket. It can get overwhelming quickly, especially with the advanced metrics now being used in these sports.

Now, during a primetime NFL broadcast, when the players are being introduced, viewers can see their Pro Football Focus (PFF) position grade, ranking their performance against other players at the same position using a formula that goes over the head of just about everyone watching.

Perhaps no events showcase our obsession with raw data more than the NFL and NBA combines, where pro hopefuls are measured in several different ways — height and weight, 40-yard dash time, bench press, broad jump, vertical leap, etc. Before these guys are even drafted, we put them through the wringer (don't forget pre-draft workouts and Pro Days) to get the whole story on them. But at the end of the day, most of it revolves around numbers.

What makes all of this even more interesting is that teams then have to figure out how to construct the most efficient teams possible within money constraints. In the NFL and NBA, teams operate under a salary cap.

In MLB, there is no direct salary cap (although there is a luxury tax), but financially, teams have different amounts they can spend (international soccer also functions in this way), meaning teams still need to be smart. Cue Billy Beane and the *Moneyball* A's, who brought this type of thinking into the mainstream.

The need for players with different positions and different skill sets naturally leads to teams forming their own strategies and playstyles, increasing the overall complexity of the sport.

Complexity is a really important word here because that's what it all comes down to. Having more statistics and more variables in the mix allows for more ways to quantify skill and overall greatness, more ways to communicate this information to fans, and more potential to craft narratives.

Sports like soccer and lacrosse have been slow to catch on in the U.S. by comparison. To the uninformed, these games can look like a bunch of running around, where sometimes people score.

There aren't as many numbers whizzing by you on a broadcast, and while they can still use many of the new ways of measuring players, these areas (like player tracking) haven't been available for very long. While these games are anything but simple, from a basic statistical standpoint, they have been put at a large disadvantage.

An increase in quantifiable and easily understood statistics seems to contribute to the popularity of our major sports. There are some other factors as well. Sport longevity was already mentioned, but career longevity is important also, allowing a sport's best and most marketable athletes to carry the sport for longer periods.

Emerging sports would also do well to ensure frequent competition, with a longer season spanning a healthy portion of the year and putting the best players and teams against each other often, which inevitably leads to rivalries. This is a problem with many Olympic sports, which seem to disappear outside of a few weeks every four years.

Overall, though, one common link among many of the less-common sports is that they have been burdened by a lack of information — stats, variables, and narratives that draw people in and keep them engaged. Outstanding performances can make some inroads but for these sports, the popularity ceiling may be capped.

ANDREW LUCK'S SUDDEN RETIREMENT SHOWS THE TOLL OF BEING A PROFESSIONAL ATHLETE

Originally published: August 28, 2019

On Saturday night, during the Indianapolis Colts third preseason game against the Chicago Bears, ESPN's Adam Schefter dropped a bomb on the football universe — Colts starting quarterback Andrew Luck was retiring.

Luck had just returned from a torn labrum which kept him out of the entire 2017 season to lead the Colts to a 10–6 record and a playoff appearance in 2018, with Luck being selected to his fourth Pro Bowl and winning Comeback Player of the Year.

Yet, after suffering another injury setback — in the form of a high-ankle issue which cost him much of the offseason and ruled him out for the preseason, Luck, at age 29, decided to call it quits.

Luck, the #1 pick in the 2012 NFL Draft, will finish his career with 23,671 passing yards, 171 passing touchdowns, and a 53–33 record as a starter. His Colts made the playoffs in each of his four Pro Bowl seasons, reaching as far as the AFC Championship Game in the 2014 season.

Jacoby Brissett, the team's starter during Luck's absence in

2017, will start for the Colts moving forward.

Luck's retirement press conference is a heartbreaking image of a man who loves his teammates and loves the game of football, but can simply no longer take the strain it puts on his body and everyday life.

In what he called the hardest decision of his life, Luck talked about a four-year cycle of pain of which there was no end in sight unless he decided to end his career. After forcing himself to play injured in 2016, he made a vow to himself never to let that happen again. Facing a similar situation now, he lived up to that promise he made himself.

He did what was best for Andrew.

At the end of the day, nothing else matters. Luck should be respected for having the courage to step away and applauded for a great career on the field. He handled everything professionally and honestly, and while he'll still be around the team he loves, Luck seems ready to enter the next phase of his life.

That is where I would love to end this article. However, if that were the case, this wouldn't be a story. Huge news, sure — but not a story. It's the mixed reaction Luck's retirement received, and my subsequent disappointment in humanity that forces me to write about it.

Andrew Luck gave everything he had for the game of football until he had nothing left to give. Unfortunately, not everyone seems to agree with the idea that people have the right to make decisions that are in their own best interest — not even his own fans.

The timing of Schefter's report created a surreal situation where Colts fans at Lucas Oil Stadium were made aware of Luck's retirement during a game where Luck was on the sidelines. Once the game was over, fans let Luck have it as he headed to the locker room.

The booing is downright despicable, especially from people who were Luck's biggest fans just hours earlier. But it doesn't surprise me in the slightest. Remember when Toronto Raptors fans cheered Kevin Durant's ruptured Achilles injury he suffered in the NBA Finals?

It's the same problem — a dehumanization of athletes by fans that see them as either mythical creatures or servants. Their feelings don't matter. No one wants to hear what they have to say. They just need to shut up and play.

People like to talk about how disloyal this generation of athletes is when they move from team to team. But after seeing what happened to Luck when he decided to step away, why would they ever feel required to have an allegiance to a city and a fanbase that won't show them a shred of decency the moment they stop performing on the field?

I understand that the announcement happened suddenly, and so close to the start of the season, but that doesn't justify this type of reaction.

In all of this, I would expect members of the media to act as the voices of reason, supporting Luck and his decision. Thankfully, most of these people have done just that. Still, people like Doug Gottlieb have only made matters worse by insinuating that Luck is "soft" for retiring when he did.

Andrew Luck said it himself — he's been in constant pain for years. And through all of that, he's still fought each and every day, playing when healthy enough, and being the leader and figurehead for a professional football team.

If you thought, for even a moment, that Andrew Luck was soft, take a look at his injury history, which includes torn cartilage in two ribs, a partially torn abdomen, a lacerated kidney, a concussion, and a torn labrum in his throwing shoulder, all before this latest ankle injury. Would you still be playing football after all of that?

I think Colts GM Chris Ballard said it best when speaking during the retirement press conference.

"For those people that booed tonight – this is an emotional night, I understand that. This young man did a lot for the city of Indianapolis. Nobody died."

Nobody died. Yet, this is what we choose to be outraged over. It remains unclear whether Luck's retirement will spark a trend of star players choosing to retire early, although we have seen a number of athletes in recent years do so. With the extreme physical toll of being a professional athlete, we should be surprised, if anything, that more athletes haven't followed in Luck's footsteps.

Just because this isn't the way it's always been doesn't mean this should be looked down upon. The right kind of change can be positive.

Athletes are much more willing to open up about their personal well-being than ever before, with Kevin Love, Liz Cambage, Michael Phelps and others leading a charge of discussing athlete mental health as it becomes a larger and more socially acceptable issue in society as a whole.

Football was obviously taking a huge toll on Luck's physical, mental, and emotional state, which is why he ultimately decided to retire. In doing so, he walks away from the $64 million left on the remaining three years of contract but gains freedom, and hopefully, peace.

It's the media's job to dissect every aspect of a story like this one, such as the fantasy football implications of Luck's retirement, and its effect on the Colts' Super Bowl odds. People will debate Luck's legacy and attempt to place the blame for Luck's injuries on various groups, from his coaches to Colts management and his offensive line. Some will even peddle conspiracy theories about Luck coming out of retirement to join the XFL, of which his father is the CEO and commissioner.

But when we do this, it only shows our lack of empathy and need to view everything in terms of how it affects us and the way we experience football. None of it gives any care to Andrew.

There does not need to be a discussion over whether Luck should have retired. Quite frankly, we don't have the right to even debate the issue. It's his decision, and because of the media, one that he wasn't even able to make on his own terms.

Still, he went up on the podium, talked us through everything, and even answered questions from the press, without ever once displaying a "why me?" attitude or claiming not to have gotten his fair shake. For that, we should all be grateful.

Commenting on a photograph taken during the press conference, Luck's former teammate Pat McAfee said, "I hope he finds his joy." Me too, Pat. Me too.

WILL THE ACC'S 20-GAME CONFERENCE SCHEDULE KILL MID-MAJOR DREAMS?

Originally published: November 14, 2019

For the 2019–20 men's college basketball season, the Atlantic Coast Conference has moved from an 18-game conference schedule to 20, joining the Big Ten, which made a similar change last season.

We've even already seen some of these extra games in action — 14 of the conference's 15 teams (everyone but Duke, who instead defeated Kansas in the Champions Classic) played a conference game in the opening week of the season, including notable matchups such as Syracuse-Virginia and North Carolina-Notre Dame.

The games generated significant interest in a sport that often doesn't gain traction until the second half of the season, even though not all coaches supported them, such as Syracuse's Jim Boeheim, who criticized the conference games to open the season as a money grab.

Plenty of fans — particularly those of smaller schools, were upset with the ACC's schedule changes for a different reason. By adding two more conference games, every team in the league receives a boost to their strength of schedule.

While there might be other reasons to make this happen, such as to preserve rivalries or increase attendance, the number one motive is clear: to get more teams into March Madness.

Maximizing teams in March Madness is incredibly valuable for both schools and their conferences, as it leads to added prestige and cold, hard cash. With only 36 at-large bids up for grabs amongst more than 300 teams, competition is fierce.

At the cut line, this means margins are thin. Having a better strength of schedule and extra opportunities to pick up quality wins against teams in Quadrants 1 and 2 of the NET rankings could be enough to push an extra ACC team or two into the field.

For fans of mid-major teams (which I define as playing in leagues other than the American [yes, the American — it's a better league than the Pac 12], ACC, Big East, Big 12, Big Ten, Pac 12, and SEC), this could rightfully come across as alarming.

Mid-majors' best chances of picking up quality wins often happen in the nonconference part of the schedule. While high-major conference teams can benefit from these extra conference games, this change wouldn't make sense for mid-majors. More conference games would only hurt their strength of schedule and add more trap games which could lead to devastating losses.

Moreover, added conference games for ACC teams could make them less likely to schedule strong mid-majors in their non-conference schedules, instead opting for guarantee games (games where high-major teams pay a fee for another team to play them at home) against weaker opponents.

As someone always rooting for more mid-majors to make the NCAA Tournament (I'm fully onboard the Evansville hype train right now), the development of 20-game conference schedules is troubling. I would expect the Pac-12, SEC, and perhaps even the American to follow suit in the coming years (with only 10 teams, the Big East and Big 12 are fairly locked into 18-game double-round robin schedules).

However, there are reasons to believe these changes will have little effect on how many mid-majors receive at-large bids to the Big Dance.

It starts with the physical makeup of the selection committee, which determines the 68-team March Madness field. The committee is comprised of 10 members who are either conference commissioners or athletic directors/vice presidents of athletics for individual schools. Committee members serve staggered five-year terms.

Traditionally, the committee has been comprised of six representatives from mid-major conferences and schools, and four from high-majors.

This balance of power was shifted in 2014 when Creighton's athletic director, Bruce Rasmussen, was elected to the committee in the same year that Creighton moved from the mid-major Missouri Valley Conference to the high-major Big East.

For five years, the committee was split 5–5 between high and mid-majors. Whether intentional or not, committee members tend to be biased towards the type of school they represent, and the numbers reflect a shift to fewer mid-major at-large bids once Rasmussen joined the committee.

From 2011 (the first year following the tournament's expansion to 68 teams) to 2013, a total of 29 mid-major teams (~9.7 per season) earned at-large bids. During Rasmussen's five-year tenure on the committee from 2014–18, that number dropped all the way down to 4.4.

Admittedly, this statistic is somewhat misleading. The American Athletic Conference, which I consider a high-major, only formed following the dissolution of the original Big East and didn't compete until Rasmussen's first year on the committee.

The American took teams from mid-major conferences such as Temple and Wichita State, while mid-majors Butler, Xavier, and Creighton joined the new Big East.

Still, even when removing the schools which now compete in high-major conferences, we're left with an average of 7 mid-major at-large bids from 2011–13 compared to 4.4 from 2014–18.

But now that Rasmussen's term has ended, there are signs of hope.

In 2019, the first year with the committee once again featuring six Mid-Major representatives, four mid-majors received at-large bids, one more than in each of the previous three seasons.

It goes beyond just the pure number of teams making the tournament, though. 2019 was another weak year for the Atlantic 10 and Mountain West, two conferences which at one point (and not too long ago, either, despite it feeling like ages) were competitive with high-major leagues.

(For example, in 2013, five teams from both the A-10 and Mountain West made March Madness. In 2019, each conference saw just two teams go dancing.)

Despite this, we saw a committee that respected mid-majors in a way we haven't seen in years. When Belmont received an at-large bid, it marked the first time since 1987 that the Ohio Valley Conference had two teams in March Madness.

The Bracket Matrix, which tracks March Madness field projections from bracketologists across the internet (and of which I am part of), had Belmont making the field in just 56 of 195 final brackets (~29%), making them the predicted third team out of the field.

Yet, the committee awarded the Bruins a play-in game, and Belmont would make good on that opportunity by beating Temple for the first tournament win in school history.

Even the first team out of the tournament was a surprise. 2019 was arguably the strongest year in the history of the Southern Conference (SoCon), with four teams finishing in the top 75 of the NET rankings (Wofford, Furman, UNC Greensboro, and East Tennessee State).

Had anyone but Wofford won the SoCon Tournament, the Terriers would have certainly received an at-large. When Wofford earned the SoCon's automatic bid, the conference's best hope of getting a second team in the field rode with UNCG.

But the odds weren't looking good. Just 8 of 195 members (~4%) of the Bracket Matrix had UNCG in their final field, making them the projected seventh team out.

The Spartans weren't even in my next four out. This isn't because I thought they weren't good, but because conferences like the SoCon hadn't been respected by the committee in recent years.

UNCG finishing as the first team left out of the tournament came as a big surprise, especially as they finished above TCU, who most expected to make the tournament.

If 2019 is any indication, it seems the committee will treat mid-majors more favorably in the future, choosing to value things teams can control (nonconference scheduling and performance in games against quality opponents) above a team's overall strength of schedule.

Extra conference games alone will not be enough to sway the selection committee to choose a particular team. Schools will need to make the most of their opportunities for quality wins while maintaining a respectable overall record.

To further explain these points, let's learn from two teams who missed the field of 68 in 2019.

North Carolina State

NC State's failure to make the tournament in 2019 has been cited as a reason for the ACC's move to a 20-game schedule.

The Wolfpack finished a solid 22–11 (9–9 ACC) with a NET ranking of 33. These numbers, particularly given that NC State plays in one of the best conferences in the nation, would normally suggest that NC State was well-deserving of a bid.

However, two things held NC State back: They played the weakest nonconference schedule in the country (353rd of 353), and despite winning nine ACC games, they went just 1–8 against the seven ACC teams that made the tournament, with that sole win coming against Syracuse, the league's seventh-best team.

On the surface, NC State looked like a tournament team. But in actuality, they hadn't beaten anyone! Two more conference games wouldn't have changed much unless NC State did something with them. An extra win over Pittsburgh and a loss to Duke would have left them in virtually the same position.

Texas

This isn't always true for NIT champions, but you could make the case that Texas was the best team left out of March Madness last season.

On Selection Sunday, every predictive metric used by the selection committee ranked the Longhorns somewhere between the high-20s and mid-30s.

Marquee wins weren't an issue, either. Texas had six Quad-1 victories, including against North Carolina, Purdue, and Kansas, who were all awarded top-four seeds in the tournament. They also had the #6 overall strength of schedule in the country.

Sure, an 8–10 record in conference play isn't ideal, but we've seen the committee overlook losing conference records before.

In this same season, another Big 12 team, Oklahoma, got in with an inferior 7–11 Big 12 record!

What's the difference here? Overall record. Oklahoma finished at 19–13, while Texas was just 16–16. Regardless of what the numbers say, the committee has never placed a .500 team in the tournament. The closest we've come was a 16–14 Georgia team in 2001 that had the top-ranked strength of schedule.

Texas was the first .500 team with a legitimate tournament argument in a while, but whether the committee doesn't believe a .500 team is deserving or wants to avoid the potential blowback from placing a 16–16 team in the field, it's clear that a certain record threshold exists for tournament inclusion, somewhere around three or four games above .500.

In the Big Ten's first season with a 20-game conference schedule, both Indiana and Nebraska both suffered brutal losing streaks that left them hovering around .500. Neither was able to show enough consistency or ability to win away from home to earn an at-large bid and they came away with disappointing seasons as a result.

20-game conference schedules are meat grinders that place immense pressure on teams to have gaudy nonconference records. This leaves teams figuring out how to balance picking up wins with avoiding becoming the next NC State.

Added conference games mean added losses for those involved. In some ways, it's easier for mid-majors if they can schedule smartly and capitalize on their opportunities to make a statement.

The ACC and Big Ten will be interesting to monitor this season, but I doubt the extra conference games will make much of a difference. If anything, the committee could be turned off by teams with 15 losses and look to give mid-majors more of a chance.

WHAT IS THE MAXIMUM NUMBER OF HOME RUNS A PLAYER CAN HIT IN A SEASON?

Originally published: November 29, 2019

2019 was a record-breaking year for home runs in Major League Baseball. Batters smashed a total of 6,776 homers, the equivalent of 1.395 long balls per team per game. 2017 is the only season that comes within even 1,000 dingers of that mark.

Given how many home runs are hit in today's game, we could once again see some huge individual home run totals. In fact, Barry Bonds' all-time record of 73 home runs in a season should be for the taking.

When it does go down, how high can the new record go? *What is the maximum number of home runs that can be hit in a season?*

First things first — how many opportunities to hit a home run can a player receive in a season? The MLB record for plate appearances in a single season belongs to Jimmy Rollins, who stepped up to the plate 778 times for the Philadelphia Phillies in 2007.

That's a good starting point, but we can't quite use that number. Rollins was a leadoff hitter, which naturally maximized his number of plate appearances. The best power hitters, on the other hand, are typically placed either third or fourth in the lineup, giving them a greater chance of hitting when players are already on base.

Barry Bonds actually was first in the batting order in 462 games during his career. However, they almost exclusively came at the beginning of his career. 1990 was the final season when Bonds batted leadoff in multiple games. To remind you, his 73 home run season came in 2001, and his streak of four consecutive National League MVPs came from 2001–04, more than a decade after he stopped batting leadoff.

During these years, Bonds batted either third or fourth in every game he started. Luckily, using the average number of plate appearances for every starter in the order, we can estimate the maximum number of times a power hitter could step up to the plate in a season.

While the first spot in the batting order gets an average of 4.65 plate appearances per game, the third spot gets 4.43, or about 95.3% as many expected plate appearances. By multiplying that rate by Rollins' record of 778 plate appearances, we can estimate the maximum number of plate appearances for a power hitter in a season to be 741.

So, there you have it — 741 is the theoretical maximum amount of home runs a player could hit in a season.

Well, not really.

If a player was able to hit a guaranteed home run on every plate appearance, teams would intentionally walk that player every time he came up in the order. After all, giving up one base is much better than four.

The statistic which describes how many bases a player gains per at-bat is slugging percentage. A perfect slugging percentage — a home run (four bases) every at-bat — would be 4.000.

While they are plate appearances, walks don't count as at-bats. Still, in terms of slugging percentage, we can think of a walk as being equivalent to a single, which earns one base and a slugging percentage of 1.000. This means that if a player's slugging percentage goes above 1.000, it makes sense for an opposing team to walk them every time.

(Note: in certain situations, such as a tie game with the bases loaded in the bottom of the ninth, our player would never be intentionally walked. That being said, for the purposes of our experiment, the 1.000 threshold makes sense to use.)

We can't have that, so we need to manage the number of home runs our optimal home run hitter hits to stay under that threshold. Given 741 plate appearances, our batter would need to hit a home run on just under one-fourth of their at-bats to avoid being walked. This puts our new maximum at 185 home runs in a season.

It's an improvement, and you could technically use this figure, but it's still unrealistic. Reaching 185 home runs in a season would require every hit by a player to result in a home run, which is impossible.

Even in the Home Run Derby, where MLB's greatest power hitters are lobbed meatballs primed to be crushed to a different zip code, plenty of balls fail to make it out of the park. It's difficult, even for the best of the best, to make consistent, perfect contact. And that's just in an exhibition environment. A professional baseball game is a different animal entirely.

What we need is an estimate of an all-time great power hitter's slugging percentage with their home runs removed. Let's go back to our friend Barry Bonds.

In 2001, Bonds posted a slugging percentage of .863, which is another all-time record. However, if you remove the 73 home runs, that figure drops to around .295.

If we give our optimal home run hitter that slugging percentage on all at-bats not resulting in home runs, we can calculate our new maximum total by solving the following equation:

$$(4x+.295(741-x))/741=1$$

This results in x equaling 141. Still, we aren't done. By this point, we've reached the maximum number of home runs for a player with 741 at-bats in a season. But that's not where we started — that 741 figure originally stood for plate appearances.

As I mentioned earlier, walks don't count as at-bats. Neither do plate appearances that end in a sacrifice bunt or sacrifice fly, the batter being hit by a pitch, or the batter being awarded first base due to interference or obstruction, although these instances make up a small minority when compared to walks.

Roughly eight percent of all MLB plate appearances end in walks, with that number slowly increasing due to the rise in the three true outcomes (home runs, walks, strikeouts). However, for power hitters, who pose more of a threat to collect multiple bases each time they're up to bat, that number rises as pitchers become more hesitant to throw in the strike zone.

For an all-time power hitter like Barry Bonds, things get simply ridiculous.

In 2001, Bonds walked 177 times, comprising more than 26% of his total plate appearances. Astonishingly, Bonds would actually walk in a higher percentage of his bats for each of the next three seasons, maxing out in 2004, when he walked 232 times, the most ever in a single season and over 37% of his plate appearances.

Even in his final season, 2007, during which he turned 43 years old, Bonds walked more than once per game.

Bonds could have decided to swing for the fences on pitches outside the strike zone, probably adding a few home runs to his total at the cost of his overall efficiency, but even that wouldn't eliminate his walks entirely. Sometimes, teams wouldn't even let Bonds swing the bat.

Bonds was intentionally walked 688 times during his career, which, along with his 762 home runs and 2,558 total walks, is another all-time record. During his 2004 season alone, Bonds was intentionally walked 120 times. For some perspective, that intentional walks number by itself would place Bonds fourth in the MLB for total walks that season.

That year, Bonds was intentionally walked with the bases empty 19 times, something which is completely unadvisable mathematically. But in 2004, the numbers didn't matter. People were scared of Barry Bonds.

These high walk totals limited Bonds' ability to record at-bats and hit homers. In fact, if all 664 of Bonds' plate appearances in 2001 resulted in at-bats, his pace of 73 home runs in 476 at-bats would have seen him hit roughly 102 home runs that season.

Extended to our maximum of 741 plate appearances for a power hitter, Bonds reaches 113.6 home runs, which is starting to get close to our 140 number.

But we can't ignore all of the plate appearances that result in official at-bats. In 2001, 71.7% of Bonds' plate appearances were at-bats. This means that instead of 741 plate appearances, we're only working with 531.

Edit the earlier equation to $4x + .295(531-x))/531 = 1$, and our final estimate for the maximum number of home runs a player can hit in a season comes out to be 101.

Depending on how you want to define what is possible, you might opt for either of the 141 or 185 figures. Still, we've at least managed to set a floor. A player hitting triple-digit home runs in a season could theoretically occur.

Will it, though? That's another question entirely.

At the beginning of this piece, I somewhat misleadingly described Bonds' 73 home run mark as for the taking. Judging by the overall totals from 2019, which saw 24% more home runs hit than in 2001, this would seem to be the case.

Yet, for a season that felt like one huge Home Run Derby, no individual player posted an earth-shattering mark. MLB's leading home run hitter in 2019 was New York Mets rookie Pete Alonso, who recorded 53 homers on the season.

This isn't to lessen Alonso's achievement — 53 is a big number, one that's been bested just 26 times in MLB history. Any time someone hits 50 home runs in a year, they've had a special season.

But still, 53 isn't up there with the all-time single-season totals. It's not even close to Bonds' 73 in 2001, Mark McGwire's 70 in 1998, or Sammy Sosa's three seasons out of four with at least 63 homers around those same years.

Babe Ruth even managed to hit 60 home runs in 1927, a season where teams only averaged .373 home runs per game. If you scale those numbers up to match the rate at which teams knocked balls out of the park in 2019, Babe Ruth managed to hit the modern equivalent of 224 home runs that season.

Of course, a number like that is laughably unattainable, but Ruth's actual total of 60, which was now set nearly a century ago, has still only been reached by four other players, and three of them — Mark McGwire, Sammy Sosa, and Bonds — were caught for using PEDs.

Because of this, some still consider Roger Maris' mark of 61 the single-season record. The fact that no one over the last 58 years has been able to match Maris while playing clean is remarkable. Players are currently hitting home runs at an almost 50%

higher rate than back then.

Even Maris' number is somewhat up for debate, as he received the benefit of his Yankees playing a modern 162-game schedule while Ruth's Yankees in 1927 played just 154 games. Through his team's first 154 games in 1961, Maris only hit 59 home runs.

Over the last century, the rise of home runs hit by the average team per game has far outpaced the marginal growth in leading annual home run totals for an individual player. This supports the idea that we've basically reached the peak of human home run hitting potential. The highest number a player can realistically hit in a single season is around 60.

The main change over time is that while the ceiling isn't getting higher, the average player has become a better power hitter. Changes in rules, playing equipment, and coaching stemming from an increased understanding of analytics have made hitting home runs easier and more common than ever before.

League leaders in any given year still hang in the 40s or perhaps even 50s, but an average player who starts most of his team's games will now finish in the low 20s, rather than the teens or even single digits of prior seasons.

So while teams are hitting more home runs than ever before, for top players, not much has changed. It might be fun to think about, but unless there are significant modifications to the way baseball is played, a player cracking 100 home runs or more in one season just isn't going to happen.

DON'T TREAT WOMEN'S SPORTS LIKE A SEPARATE CATEGORY

Originally published: December 6, 2019

Women's sports are in a better place than ever before, with greater access to participation, and visible role models such as those found on the U.S. Women's National Soccer Team or in the WNBA.

That being said, there is still a long way to go to achieve gender equality. Among the remaining issues, U.S. Soccer continues to fight against equal pay for the USWNT, TV coverage of women's sports is limited, declining, and delivered differently than men's sports, and merchandise is almost impossible to find, even in-market for championship teams.

Fixing these issues will require some changes in the leadership of sports organizations and media companies. In addition, women need to be afforded more opportunities on the business side of sports.

Time is another important factor. There was a point when women were not allowed to participate in many sports at all. Undoubtedly, public opinion on the value of women's sports will continue to progress, even if not at the speed many of us would like.

But perhaps we also need to reframe the way women's sports are classified and named.

It may be convenient to group women's sports together and discuss them as a whole, but doing so turns gender into a niche, making women's sports seem less important than men's.

This gives a license to critics who claim they don't like women's sports or don't find them interesting. These ideas are absurd. Women's basketball, gymnastics, and snowboarding couldn't be more different. The only linking characteristic is the gender of those competing. For someone who considers themselves a fan of other sports to give a blanket statement suggesting they don't care for an entire gender's sporting catalog isn't preference—it's sexism.

No one ever discusses men's sports as a whole—the scope is too large, and the concept is unnecessary. The same should be true for women's sports. As it currently stands, women's sports are grouped together and treated in a similar fashion as the action sports and esports niches of which many are unsure should be called sports at all.

For example, ESPN has a women-specific page and corresponding social media accounts focusing on women in sports called espnW. The concept of espnW is tricky—on one hand, it's great to have these sports and athletes receiving coverage.

But at the same time, it lumps all of women's sports together and pushes it to a sister site. Very rarely does women's sports content appear on ESPN's main page. In fact, espnW's existence might just be akin to ticking a box in order to justify a lack of coverage in other places.

Women's sports should be covered not to appease people, but rather because these sports are equally respected. In a perfect world, gender would be irrelevant when discussing a sports competition. That world can be made a reality by talking about women's sports simply because they exist, not because we're required to push them.

The concept of women's sports being classified in ways that undermine their popularity and present them as below men's sports extends to the names of leagues and organizations themselves. That the WNBA and NWSL include the word "women's" in their names implicitly conveys they are below the NBA and MLS, which don't need a gender qualifier.

It goes beyond just those two sports. In golf, men play on the PGA Tour, while ladies play on the LPGA Tour. Men's tennis is governed by the Association of Tennis Professionals (ATP), while the female equivalent is the Women's Tennis Association (WTA).

With their naming, the WNBA and LPGA, in particular, come across as subsidiaries to the male versions of their sports in a similar way to how the Junior Olympics and Paralympics are part of the Olympic movement but not the main event.

Admittedly, this is difficult to change, as leagues have existent branding. That being said, NPF (National Pro Fastpitch) succeeded in changing its name from the Women's Pro Softball League and should be applauded.

Even down to team names, the female sports teams of many schools are known as the "lady" version of the school's nickname. Similarly, women's professional teams often use conceptual names as Dream, Liberty, or Courage, which convey a less competitive atmosphere in comparison to more aggressive names such as Bears, Raiders, or Raptors that can be found in men's sports.

Certainly, the beliefs of both those in power and many everyday citizens are barriers on the road to true equality for women's sports. But beyond ideology, taxonomic issues have turned gender into a niche, almost guaranteeing women play second fiddle in the sports landscape.

BEYOND THE STREAK: THE IRON MEN OF SPORTS

Originally published: December 22, 2019

They say the best ability is availability. If that's the case, the athletes presented here are the most valuable players of all. These lineup staples seldom sat—some never missed a game in their entire careers. In fact, they suited up so regularly for such an extended period of time that just by showing up to work, their names are etched in the record books. They are the iron men, and here are their streaks.

An ironman streak is different from all other types of streaks. Whereas most streaks measure performance achievements such as games won in a row or consecutive all-star appearances, to maintain an ironman streak, all one needs to do is play in every one of their team's games.

On the surface, that might not seem very difficult. However, ironman streaks command the highest respect from players and fans alike—and for good reason. To achieve one of these records, a player must first be in their league for a long time, which itself is quite an accomplishment. Then, the player must be good enough to receive playing time in every game without getting hurt or being unavailable for any reason.

The ironman streak doesn't care if your first child is being born or if one of your parents just passed away. It doesn't care if you're exhausted after a long road trip or if you have the flu. You have to play in every single game year after year just to have a chance.

This is easier to do in some sports than others. Looking at the most recently completed seasons for the Big 4 North American sports leagues (the NFL, NBA, MLB, and NHL), the NFL actually saw the highest proportion of players playing every game of the regular season. Of all 2,150 players who played at least one game, 677 played 16 games. That amounts to 31.49%.

Of course, this isn't to say that football is safer than other sports —the difference here comes from the smaller amount of games and longer time in between games in the NFL regular season. That more than two-thirds of players miss games is incredibly alarming. Yet, that number is still higher in other leagues.

In the NHL, just 106 of 906 skaters (11.7%) played all 82 games in the 2018–19 season. In the NBA, that number is 21 of 530 or 3.96%. However, Major League Baseball, with its grueling 162-game schedule, sees the fewest number of players compete in every game. In 2019, only 5 of 635 position players managed to play in every game. That amounts to .79%.

Not only does the sport one is playing affect their ironman potential—their position does as well. Five out of 635 position players played all 162 games in the MLB last season. I make the distinction of position players because there's no point in counting pitchers.

A pitcher will never play in 162 games—it's just impossible. In 2019, Álex Claudio, with 83 appearances, was the only pitcher to pitch in even half of his team's games. The record for most games pitched in a season is 106, set by Mike Marshall in 1974 with the Dodgers. That same season, he set the modern record with 13 consecutive games pitched, which has since been tied by the Rangers' Dale Mohorcic in 1986.

To find the all-time record for most consecutive games pitched, though, we have to go back to the founding of the National

League in 1876. That year, Jim Devlin, pitching for the Louisville Grays, started 68 straight games, only missing their 69th and final game of the year.

The following season, Devlin, as the only pitcher on the Grays' roster, pitched all 61 games and all 559 innings for the team. Following that 1877 campaign, Devlin and three of his teammates were issued lifetime bans for accepting money to throw games late in the season. Still, Devlin's 1877 season is and forever will be the only time a pitcher will have played in every game in a year.

Due to the time in which it was set, Devlin's record is unbreakable. Another of these such records belongs to the NHL goaltender Glenn Hall, who started 502 consecutive regular season games in net from 1955–62.

For a casual observer, it may seem like goaltenders would be able to play every game when healthy, similar to goalkeepers in soccer. For example, while Frank Lampard holds the record for most consecutive Premier League matches played for an outfield player with 164, Brad Friedel more than doubled that as a goalkeeper with 310 straight appearances from 2004–12.

With hockey, it's the opposite. While 502 consecutive games played is the record for goaltenders, the overall record is 964, set by Doug Jarvis from 1975–87.

Playing goalie in hockey is incredibly exhausting. While a skater (aka non-goalie) might be on the ice for 20 minutes per game, goalies are out there for all 60. They face both the physical challenges of being in the correct position and saving shots and the mental challenge of staying hyper-focused for an entire game. Furthermore, with their heavy padding, goalies frequently lose several pounds of pure sweat during a game.

For all of these reasons, NHL teams typically frequently mix a second and sometimes even a third goaltender into their rotations. Last season, Devan Dubnyk of the Minnesota Wild led all goalies with 67 games played out of a possible 82.

Back when Glenn Hall played, seasons were only 70 games long, meaning his streak of 502 lasted over seven full seasons. In the 82-game era, no player has played in every game of even a single season, with Grant Fuhr's 79 games in 1995–96 topping the list. Oh, and by the way—Hall's streak came before goalies wore masks.

In basketball, a player's position doesn't have a major impact on his ability to play a full 82 games, as all players perform similar actions while on the court. While guards are the most represented, the list of the 21 players who played in every game last season includes multiple players from each position. Big men may be more susceptible to certain kinds of injuries, but even Yao Ming played 82 games in each of his first two seasons in the league. Perhaps it takes a larger toll on taller players over time, but there are still examples of taller players who stayed remarkably healthy.

In fact, the NBA's iron man record holder is the 6'9" A.C. Green, who played 1,192 straight games between 1986 and his retirement in 2001. He missed just three games in his entire career.

But it's more than just Green. Karl Malone, the 6'9" power forward and second-leading scorer in NBA history, missed no more than two games in any season and only 10 total games during the first 18 years of his 19-year career. Also standing 6'9", Red Kerr played 844 straight games back in the 50s and 60s, and Elvin Hayes missed just 9 games in 16 seasons. Like Malone, he never missed more than two in a year.

The 6'10" Tristan Thompson played in 447 straight games for the Cavaliers between 2012 and 2017 and had the NBA's longest active ironman streak at the time. Finally, both standing at least seven feet tall, Kareem Abdul-Jabbar and Robert Parish both missed remarkably few games in careers spanning 20 and 21 seasons, respectively.

The NFL is similarly diverse in terms of positions with ironman streaks. Of the 25 players with the most consecutive games played, 13 are special teams players, while six played offense and six played defense. (For our purposes, George Blanda, who also played quarterback for much of his career, counts as a kicker, and John Hadl, who punted early in his career, counts as a quarterback.)

Quarterbacks, tight ends, offensive linemen, all three levels of the defense, kickers, punters, and long snappers are all represented with streaks of at least 224 regular season games, the equivalent of fourteen 16-game seasons. The only notable exceptions are running backs and wide receivers, skill positions where long-term durability is more difficult.

But which NFL player has the most consecutive games played? I'll give you a hint—it's not who you think. The name which should immediately come to mind is Brett Favre. Favre owns one of the most famous ironman streaks of all-time, starting 297 straight games at quarterback for the Packers, Jets, and Vikings from Week 4 of the 1992 season through Week 13 of the 2010 season.

This is indeed the record for most consecutive starts in the NFL. However, technically, only 22 players "start" a football game—11 on offense and 11 on defense. Special teamers aren't included. Punter Jeff Feagles played 22 seasons in the NFL from 1988 to 2009 and never once missed a game. With 352 consecutive regular season games played, Feagles is the NFL's ultimate ironman, although I think we'd all agree that Favre's consecutive start mark is more impressive.

Favre's streak is incredible—as are Doug Jarvis', A.C. Green's, and every other player mentioned thus far. However, one ironman streak stands above all the rest—one so absurd that the player to have accomplished it is nicknamed "The Iron Man." This record, like Jim Devlin's and Glenn Hall's, is unbeatable. However, this isn't due to any changes in the game.

Less than one percent of MLB position players played 162 games in 2019. That number stays consistent throughout the 1980s and 90s when baseball's ultimate ironman streak took place. Yet, despite those long odds of playing every game of just one season, Cal Ripken Jr. managed to do it.

Then he did it again. And again. And again. And again. And again. And again. And again. And again. And again. And again. And again. And again. And again. And again. And again.

2,632 games. Cal Ripken Jr. played in 2,632 straight games for the Baltimore Orioles, the equivalent of over sixteen 162-game seasons. From May 30, 1982, to September 20, 1998, if the Orioles were playing baseball, so was Ripken.

And these weren't just pinch-hitting appearances, either. Within the 2,632 consecutive games played there is another ironman record—8,243 consecutive innings played, a mark lasting 904 games and only ending when Ripken was subbed out in the bottom of the eighth inning of a blowout.

Ripken is far more than just a consecutive games streak—he made the All-Star Game 19 times, won two MVPs, is a member of the 3,000 hit club, and was a first-ballot Hall of Famer. Still, to many, he'll forever be known as that guy that seemingly went a lifetime without missing a baseball game.

To give you an idea of how difficult it is to play in 2,632 straight games, here are just a few of the obstacles Ripken faced along the way. On July 26, 1993, Ripken's son Ryan was born. The Orioles played 26 games in July of 1993. The 26th was an off day.

Ripken played with a severely twisted knee, multiple ankle injuries, and a broken nose. After the 1994 MLB season ended early due to a player strike, the league was dangerously close to having to use replacement players to start the 1995 season. Doing so would have ended Ripken's streak, but a deal was reached just days before the season had been initially scheduled to start. On opening day for the Orioles, Ripken could be found at shortstop, his usual spot.

The previous high for consecutive games played in the MLB was 2,130, set by Yankees legend Lou Gehrig in 1939. For decades, people considered Gehrig's mark to be one that would never be surpassed. Ripken did the unthinkable—he broke an unbreakable record. Perhaps the only thing as surprising as Ripken topping Gehrig is the way both men's streaks ended.

So—how does an ironman streak end? Every streak has to be snapped one way or another, and for the ironman streak, there are five ways it can happen.

The first of these ways is retirement. At some point, typically at the end of a season, an older player can decide that enough is enough. In this case, the streak arguably never really ends—instead, it goes on more of a permanent hiatus. This was the case for both the NBA and NFL consecutive games played leaders, A.C. Green and Jeff Feagles.

Then, there's a physical inability to play, accounting for both injury and illness. This is likely the most common way a serious ironman streak ends. Injuries notably derailed the ironman streaks of quarterbacks Brett Favre (297 straight starts) and Peyton Manning (208 straight starts). Frank Lampard's record for consecutive Premier League appearances fell due to illness.

Another player who saw their ironman streak meet an injury-caused demise was Joe Thomas, the legendary Cleveland Browns offensive tackle. From the time Thomas was drafted in 2007 until the Browns' matchup against the Titans in Week 7 of the 2017 season, not only had he started every single game for the Browns—he hadn't missed a single offensive play.

But that streak finally ended when Thomas tore his triceps in that game against the Titans. The injury prematurely ended Thomas' season, and in the offseason, the 33-year old decided to call it a career. His 10,363 consecutive snaps played in 167 games remain an NFL record.

The third way an ironman streak can end is if a player is benched, and this has led to some interesting stories. Joe Thomas owns the record for consecutive snaps played with 10,363, but it's another offensive tackle, drafted a year before Thomas in 2006, who should probably own that record.

D'Brickashaw Ferguson played in all 160 regular-season games for the Jets during his 10-year career. He played a total of 10,707 snaps, a number higher than Thomas. The only problem? He missed one snap in the middle of it all. And it wasn't due to injury, either.

During the final week of the 2008 season, the Jets trailed the Dolphins by a touchdown with seven seconds left. In possession of the ball at their own four-yard line, the Jets attempted to play the lateral game. For this, they sent out their most athletic group of players possible. The 310-pound Ferguson was not among them.

Taking his place at left tackle, of all people, was cornerback Darrelle Revis. The play failed, as most laterals do, and Ferguson's consecutive snaps streak was, well, snapped. He wouldn't miss another play in his final seven years in the league.

A quarterback the Jets would draft five years later would go on to end another legendary ironman streak. When Geno Smith started for the New York Giants in favor of a benched Eli Manning in Week 13 of 2017, it snapped Manning's streak of 210 consecutive starts for the Giants dating back to 2004. The day after Smith's start, the Giants fired both their head coach and general manager, and Eli Manning returned to his starting position.

Red Kerr was the victim of another pointless benching. The NBA's original iron man was playing for the Baltimore Bullets in what would be his 12th and final season and holding on to a streak of 844 consecutive games played since he entered the league, when his coach, a former teammate named Paul Seymour, inexplicably decided to sit Kerr for a game. According to Seymour, the streak had to end sometime, and the longer it persisted, the more of a distraction it would present to the team. Just like that, Kerr's streak was over.

The NHL's all-time leader in consecutive games played was benched as well. Some will say that Doug Jarvis never missed a game during his NHL career. This is technically true, as Jarvis played in all 964 games in which he was on an NHL roster.

However, following what would be the final game in his streak, Jarvis was sent down from the Hartford Whalers to the team's AHL developmental team, the Binghamton Whalers. There, Jarvis played a final 24 games before retiring. So yes, Jarvis never missed a game, but he also didn't finish his career in the NHL.

Getting sent to the minor leagues as your league's all-time ironman record holder is bad, but it isn't the worst way for a streak to end. That would be suspension, which has happened more often than you'd think.

The fourth-longest ironman streak in NHL history belongs to Andrew Cogliano, who went over 10 years after entering the league without missing a game. Fewer than two seasons away from history, Cogliano's streak ended at 830 games after an illegal hit resulted in a two-game suspension.

In the NBA, Andre Miller lost a 634-game streak in 2010 after he was issued a flagrant-two post-game for intentionally slamming into Blake Griffin in a move missed by the officials initially. A couple of years earlier, Bruce Bowen's 500-game ironman streak came to an end when he was suspended for kicking

Chris Paul.

Even in NASCAR, Matt Kenseth's streak of 571 consecutive starts, the longest active at the time and spanning over 15 years, ended in 2015 when he was given a two-race ban for intentionally crashing into Joey Logano.

All of this brings us to the final way to end an ironman streak: voluntary absence. Cal Ripken Jr. played in 2,632 straight MLB games. Lou Gehrig achieved 2,130 in a row. No other player in league history has more than 1,307. So, how did these two legends' streaks come to a close? It's simple—they said so.

On the day of the Orioles' final home game of 1998, Ripken simply walked into manager Ray Miller's office and said he wanted to sit out. For the greatest ironman streak of them all, that was that. Ripken was given a standing ovation—it was important to him that the streak ended in front of a home crowd. He would go on to play three more seasons before retiring at the age of 41, after 21 seasons with the Orioles.

Sadly, Lou Gehrig's streak doesn't have the same happy ending. Having underperformed in the early goings of the 1939 season and still suffering from back pains which had been later diagnosed and treated as a gall bladder condition, Gehrig said it wouldn't be fair to the team, his manager, the fans, or himself for him to play.

According to manager Joe McCarthy, "Lou just told me he felt it would be best for the club if he took himself out of the line-up. I asked him if he really felt that way. He told me he was serious. He feels blue. He is dejected."

Covering the event for the New York Times, James P. Dawson wrote the following:

"Gehrig's withdrawal from today's game does not necessarily mean the end of his playing career, although that seems not far distant. When that day comes Gehrig can sit back and enjoy the fortune he has accumulated as a ball player."

But Gehrig never got that chance. Further testing showed what was thought to be a gall bladder condition was actually Amyotrophic lateral sclerosis, now known as ALS or Lou Gehrig's disease. He would never play another game, and with his health rapidly deteriorating, Gehrig passed away in June of 1941, just two years after his last MLB appearance.

As something of a midpoint between Ripken's playing of three more seasons and Gehrig's retirement, NASCAR's iron man king Jeff Gordon ended his streak of 797 consecutive starts when after the 2015 season, he stopped racing full-time. Gordon would still make eight starts the following year in place of an injured Dale Earnhardt Jr. before his moving on from racing in NASCAR.

Randy Smith, the holder of the NBA's second-longest ironman streak, also saw his run end due to voluntary absence, albeit in a unique situation. After playing in 906 games in a row, Smith requested to be placed on waivers by the Clippers in order to move to a playoff contender. From his final Clippers game, it was only five days until he suited up for the Hawks. However, since he missed a game during the time it took to clear waivers, the NBA ruled his streak over.

Smith could have rooted against anyone breaking his record, still upset over the NBA's ruling, but he didn't. The ironman club is special because of the unparalleled commitment it requires to become a member—something only a select few players have experienced. When A.C. Green played his 907th straight game to set a new record, Smith was in the stands, cheering him on. Know who else was there? Cal Ripken Jr.

From Smith, Green, and Ripken to Jim Devlin, Glenn Hall, Brett Favre, and all the others, the iron men of sports took simply playing in games—something we take for granted—and turned it into an art. For their dedication, their achievements are set in stone.

ABOUT THE AUTHOR

Connor Groel is an up-and-coming sportswriter from The Woodlands, Texas who is set to graduate from The University of Texas at Austin with a degree in sport management in May 2020. He is the owner of the Medium publication Top Level Sports, which he originally started on Blogger in 2014. Additionally, he hosts the Connor Groel Sports podcast. Connor has a passion for learning new things and enjoys listening to music, playing poker, and games of all kinds.

Twitter.com/ConnorGroel
Medium.com/@ConnorGroel

Made in the USA
Columbia, SC
24 January 2020